SCENES

for

Acting and Directing

SCENES

for
Acting and Directing

by
Samuel Elkind

Editorial Development: Paula Rene Hoffman

Typeset and Design Layout: Sharon Gorrell

PLAYERS PRESS
P.O. Box 1132
Studio City, California 91614
U.S.A.

A.C.T.
AUSTRALIA

Essex
UNITED KINGDOM

SCENES for Acting and Directing

© Copyright, 1992, by Samuel Elkind and
PLAYERS PRESS, Inc.
ISBN 0-88734-1617-0
Library of Congress Catalog Number: 91-52952

PLAYERS PRESS, Inc.
P.O. Box 1132
Studio City, CA 91614-0132, U.S.A.

Library of Congress Cataloging-in-Publication Data

Scenes for acting and directing / [compiled] by Samuel Elkind.
      p.   cm.
   ISBN 0-88734-617-0 : $16.95
   1. Acting. 2. Theater--Production and direction.   I. Elkind,
Samuel.
PN2080.S25   1991
792'.028--dc20   91-52952
                                                    CIP

Printed in U.S.A.
Simultaneously Published in U.S.A., U.K. and Australia

ACKNOWLEDGMENTS

From AH WILDERNESS! by Eugene O'Neill. Copyright 1933 and renewed 1961 by Carlotta Monterey O'Neill. Reprinted by permission of Random House, Inc., Jonathan Cape Ltd., and the Executors of the Estate of Eugene O'Neill.

From ALL MY SONS by Arthur Miller. Copyright © 1947 by Arthur Miller. Reprinted by permission of the Viking Press, Inc. and Elaine Green Ltd.

From ANTIGONE, by Jean Anouilh, edited and translated by Lewis Galantiere. Copyright 1946 by Random House, Inc. Reprinted by permission of the publisher, Random House, Inc. and Dr. Jan Van Loewen Ltd. All performing rights are controlled by Dr. Jan Van Loewen Ltd. with the exception of the American rights for the U.S.A. and Canada which are controlled by Samuel French, Inc.

From THE BARRETTS OF WIMPOLE STREET by Rudolf Besier. Copyright 1930, 1958, by Rudolf Besier. Reprinted by permission of Little, Brown and Co. and Curtis Brown Ltd.

From THE CHALK GARDEN, by Enid Bagnold. Copyright © 1953, as an unpublished work, by Enid Bagnold. Copyright © 1956, by Enid Bagnold. Copyright © 1956, Acting Edition Revised, by Enid Bagnold. Reprinted by permission of Random House, Inc. and Samuel French.

From EDWARD, MY SON, by Robert Morley and Noel Langley. Copyright 1948 by Robert Morley and Noel Langley. Reprinted by permission of Random House, Inc. and Samuel French Ltd.

From THE ENCHANTED by Jean Giraudoux, translated and adapted by Maurice Valency. Copyright 1933 by Editions Bernard Grasset (under the title INTERMEZZO) in the French language. Copyright 1948, by Maurice Valency (under the title INTERMEZZO by Jean Giraudoux). English version by Maurice Valency, Copyright, 1950 by Maurice Valency. Reprinted by permission of Random House, Inc.

From GENERATION by William Goodhart. Copyright © 1964, 1966 by William Goodhart. Reprinted by permission of Doubleday & Company, Inc.

From THE LITTLE FOXES, by Lillian Hellman. Copyright 1939 and renewed 1967 by Lillian Hellman. Reprinted by permission of Random House, Inc.

From THE MAN WHO CAME TO DINNER, by George S. Kaufman and Moss Hart. Copyright 1939 and renewed 1967 by Catherine Carlisle Hart. Reprinted by permission of Random House, Inc., and Cohen & Crossberg.

From OF THEE I SING, by George S. Kaufman and Morrie Ryskind. Copyright 1931, 1932 and renewed 1959 by George SW. Kaufman and Morrie Ryskind. Reprinted by permission of Alfred A. Knopf, Inc.

From THIEVE'S CARNIVAL by Jean Anouilh. Copyright 1952, by Jean Anouilh and Lucienne Hill. Reprinted by permission of Dr. Jan Van Loewen Ltd.

PHOTOS

GENERATION, Bolton (Henry Fonda), Doris (Holly Turner), and   Cover
   Walter (Richard Jordan), William-Alan Landes Collection

THE LITTLE FOXES Horace (Peter Donat)   Cover
   Courtesy of the American Conservatory Theatre, San Francisco, CA

A RAISIN IN THE SUN Walter (Sidney Poitier) and Beneatha (Diana Sands)   Cover
   Author's Collection

THE CHALK GARDEN   xii
   Courtesy of the American Conservatory Theatre, San Francisco, CA

THE CHALK GARDEN   29
   Courtesy of the American Conservatory Theatre, San Francisco, CA

THE CHALK GARDEN   29
   Courtesy of the American Conservatory Theatre, San Francisco, CA

THE LITTLE FOXES   40
   William-Alan Landes Collection

THE LITTLE FOXES   43
   William-Alan Landes Collection

A RAISIN IN THE SUN   74
   Author's Collection

EDWARD, MY SON   101
   Courtesy of Robert Morley

GENERATION   132
   William-Alan Landes Collection

GENERATION   139
   William-Alan Landes Collection

THE BARRETTS OF WIMPOLE STREET   143
   Author's Collection

THE BARRETTS OF WIMPOLE STREET   143
   Author's Collection

THE BARRETTS OF WIMPOLE STREET   155
   Author's Collection

GENERATION Bolton (Henry Fonda) and Walter (Richard Jordan)   Back Cover
   William-Alan Landes Collection

(All A.C.T. photos courtesy of Dennis Powers.)

CONTENTS

Scene   Page

from **ALL MY SONS**, Act 1
   Arthur Miller   1M, 1F   1

from **ALL MY SONS**, Act 2
   Arthur Miller   2M   5

from **DEEP ARE THE ROOTS**, Act 3,
   Arnaud D'Usseau and James Gow   1M, 1F, 2 Sup.   8

from **AH, WILDERNESS!**, Act 4, Scene 2
   Eugene O'Neill   1M, 1F   15

from **THE CHALK GARDEN**, Act 1
   Enid Bagnold   2F   25

from **THE CHALK GARDEN**, Act 1
   Enid Bagnold   2F, 1 Sup.   30

from **THE LITTLE FOXES**, Act 3
   Lillian Hellman   1M, 1F   36

from **THE LITTLE FOXES**, Act 3
   Lillian Hellman   2F   42

from **LADIES IN RETIREMENT**, Act 1, scene 2
   Edward Percy and Reginald Denham   2F, 2 Sup.   46

from **LADIES IN RETIREMENT**, Act 3, scene 1
   Edward Percy and Reginald Denham   1M, 1F   52

from **STAGE DOOR**, Act 1, scene 2
Edna Ferber and George S. Kaufman   2F   58

from **STAGE DOOR**, Act 1, scene 2
Edna Ferber and George S. Kaufman   2F, 1 Sup.   63

from **A RAISIN IN THE SUN**, Act 1, scene 1
Lorraine Hansberry   3F   67

from **A RAISIN IN THE SUN**, Act 3
Lorraine Hansberry   1M, 1F   75

from **THE OLD MAID**, First episode
Zoe Akins   2F   81

from **THE OLD MAID**, First episode
Zoe Akins   2F   81

from **THIEVES' CARNIVAL**, Act 3
Jean Anouilh   1M, 1F, 2 Sup.   85

from **THIEVES' CARNIVAL**, Act 3
Jean Anouilh   1M, 1F   88

from **EDWARD, MY SON**, Act 2, scene 3
Robert Morley and Noel Langley   1M, 1F   95

from **THE ENCHANTED**, Act 3
Jean Giraudoux   2M, 1F   102

from **THE HEIRESS**, Act 1, scene 3
Ruth and Augustus Goetz   2M, 1F   112

from **ANTIGONE**
    Jean Anouilh   1M, 1F   116

from **ANTIGONE**
    Jean Anouilh   1M, 1F   120

from **OF THEE I SING**, Act 1, scene 3
    George S. Kaufman and Morrie Ryskind   1M, 1F   124

from **THE MAN WHO CAME TO DINNER**, Act 1, scene 2
    Moss Hart and George S. Kaufman   1M, 1F   128

from **GENERATION**, Act 1
    William Goodhart   2M, 1F   133

from **THE BARRETTS OF WIMPOLE STREET**, Act 1
    Rudolf Besier   1M, 2F, 8 Sup.   142

from **THE BARRETTS OF WIMPOLE STREET**, Act 4
    Rudolf Besier   1M, 2F   150

from **THE BARRETTS OF WIMPOLE STREET**, Act 5, scene 1
    Rudolf Besier   1M, 1F   156

INTRODUCTION

As a growing number of students select drama courses, the demand for scenes for acting and directing practice grows proportionately. Great stress is being placed on the many learning experiences inherent in dramatic dialogue. Teachers, continually searching for worthwhile dramatic materials, rarely have sufficient time or facilities to meet these student needs. This series was compiled to help satisfy these needs.

At the same time, the scenes in this collection serve another purpose. Teachers have learned that acting exercises provide students opportunities for self-discovery and also offer them rich fields for the exploration of personality. Experience in acting out becomes a way of thinking through, for it puts the student inside the behavior of others so as to understand motivating forces in operation. An actor studies the human condition; his subject material is the human heart and the human mind. Portraying and directing the emotions, problems, and conflicts of well-drawn characters is an exercise in empathy and, as a result, the young person frequently is able to learn more about himself.

Chosen for classroom or workshop use, the scenes come from a wide variety of plays and generally focus on critical moments when important ideas, actions, and/or character revelations take place. The time, the basic setting of the action, and the general background necessary for understanding character motivation have been included in the brief introductions to the scenes. In many instances the students will want to read the entire play.

The marginal questions and comments are intended only as suggestions to help students work independently. The language is non-technical; the only technical distinction which is made is between the words "gesture" and "movement." The former indicates a physical action usually involving only a limb or the head. "Movement" indicates a change in attitude or position of the entire body. A note will also sometimes identify a character who is mentioned but does not appear in a scene. Occasionally a note will suggest an alternate beginning or end to a scene. Since these notes are neither prescriptive nor directional, the teacher/director will provide the additional guidance, direction, and assistance in solving problems which may emerge, contributing exercises as needed in developing physical coordination, concentration, imagination, flexibility of vocal patterns, etc.

Attention should be paid to the essential requirements of the stage setting. Students are encouraged to be creative in such matters as properties and set. Adequate acting space, classroom or stage, should be provided.

The scenes in this collection are primarily for growth and development; they are not intended to be polished theatrical performances for an audience. They are for practice but, a meticulously rehearsed scene may well be used for the basis of an audition piece. Thoroughly studied, blocked, and rehearsed the scenes will not only provide insight into human life and human behavior, they will also afford students the chance to create believable characters, to improve communicative skills, and to enjoy a cooperative aesthetic endeavor.

Courtesy of the American Conservatory Theatre. **The Chalk Garden** (l to r) Mrs. St. Maugham (Mirrian Walters) and Miss Madrigal (Barbara Dirickson).

AUTHOR

Dr. Elkind is a professional producer-director and an internationally acclaimed educator. He has produced, directed and moderated Specials, Talk Shows and Panel Programs for television and radio. In theatre, on a variety of stages, he has directed over 100 productions ranging from the classics to the contemporaries.

As an educator, Dr. Elkind has taught professionals, teachers and students at various levels. He has conducted and directed theatre productions and workshops, Educational and University programs in England, Scotland, Australia and throughout Italy. He has been president of the California Educational Theatre Association, Director of the High School Drama Workshop at California State University, San Francisco, and consultant to the State Department of Education for California.

Articles by Dr. Elkind have appeared in *Dramatics, The Speech Teacher,* and the *CTA Journal.* He is co-author of the *Drama/Theatre Framework for California Public Schools.* This book of scenes is the first of four books, by Dr. Elkind, to be published by Players Press for their Workshop Series.

Samuel Elkind has received an Outstanding Program Award for his television show *HELP*, and Outstanding Achievement Awards from American Theatre Association, California Educational Theatre and National Endowment for the Arts and Humanities.

Dr. Elkind received his doctorate from Columbia University and his Bachelors and Masters from San Francisco State University. He has completed advanced theatre work at Stanford University and City University of New York.

from
ALL MY SONS
ACT 1
Arthur Miller

The scene takes place in the back yard of an upper middle-class American home. There are a bench and lawn chairs.

Chris Keller has recently returned to the home of his parents, Joe and Kate Keller, after duty as a combat pilot in World War II. Visiting the Kellers for the first time in several years is Ann Deever. Ann's father, who had been Joe Keller's business partner, is serving a prison sentence for manufacturing defective airplane parts which subsequently caused the deaths of more than twenty combat fliers. Ann had been engaged to Chris's brother, Larry, who was also a pilot. Though Larry has been missing in action for nearly three years, his mother tenaciously refuses to accept the probability of his death. Learning that Ann had long ago stopped waiting for Larry's return, and suspecting that Chris and Ann are planning to marry, Mrs. Keller's attitude toward Ann has quickly cooled. Despite his wife's apprehensions, Joe Keller is delighted with Ann's presence and plans a celebration in her honor. As the following scene opens, Joe has just gone off after complimenting Ann's beauty. Chris and Ann are alone in the yard.

CHRIS (*calling after him*). Drink your tea, Casanova.[1] (*He turns to* ANN.) Isn't he a great guy?
ANN. You're the only one I know who loves his parents.
CHRIS. I know. It went out of style, didn't it?
ANN (*with a sudden touch of sadness*). It's all right. It's a good thing. (*She looks about.*) You know? It's lovely here. The air is sweet.
CHRIS (*hopefully*). You're not sorry you came?[2]
ANN. Not sorry, no. But I'm . . . not going to stay. . . .

1. Chris's call to his father may be omitted, thus beginning the scene with his words to Ann.

2. What stage area would be most appropriate to the

mood of the scene?
In what follows
when would Chris
and Ann be close?
When would they be
apart?

CHRIS. Why?

ANN. In the first place, your mother as much as told me to go.

CHRIS. Well . . .

ANN. You saw that . . . and then you . . . you've been kind of . . .

CHRIS. What?

ANN. Well . . . kind of embarrassed ever since I got here.

CHRIS. The trouble is I planned on kind of sneaking up on you over a period of a week or so. But they take it for granted that we're all set.

ANN. I knew they would. Your mother anyway.[3]

CHRIS. How did you know?

ANN. From *her* point of view, why else would I come?

CHRIS. Well . . . would you want to? (**ANN** *still studies him.*) I guess you know this is why I asked you to come.

ANN. I guess this is why I came.

CHRIS. Ann, I love you. I love you a great deal. (*Finally.*) I love you. (*Pause. She waits.*) I have no imagination . . . that's all I know to tell you. (**ANN,** *waiting, ready.*) I'm embarrassing you. I didn't want to tell it to you here. I wanted some place we'd never been; a place where we'd be brand new to each other. . . . You feel it's wrong here, don't you? This yard, this

chair? I want you to be ready for me. I don't want to win you away from anything.[4]

ANN (*putting her arms around him*). Oh, Chris, I've been ready a long, long time!

CHRIS. Then he's gone forever. You're sure.

ANN. I almost got married two years ago.

CHRIS. . . . why didn't you?

ANN. You started to write to me. . . .

(*Slight pause.*)[5]

5. How does the
pause affect the
mood of the scene?

CHRIS. You felt something that far back?

ANN. Every day since!

CHRIS. Ann, why didn't you let me know?[6]

ANN. I was waiting for you, Chris. Till then you never wrote. And when you did, what did you say? You sure can be ambiguous, you know.

CHRIS (*he looks toward house, then at her, trembling*).[7] Give me a kiss, Ann. Give me a . . . (*They kiss.*)[8] God, I kissed you, Annie, I kissed Annie. How long, how long I've been waiting to kiss you!

ANN. I'll never forgive you. Why did you wait all these years? All I've done is sit and wonder if I was crazy for thinking of you.

CHRIS. Annie, we're going to live now! I'm going to make you so happy. (*He kisses her, but without their bodies touching.*)

ANN (*a little embarrassed*). Not like that you're not.[9]

CHRIS. I kissed you. . . .

ANN. Like Larry's brother. Do it like you, Chris.[10] (*He breaks away from her abruptly.*)[11] What is it, Chris?

CHRIS. Let's drive some place . . . I want to be alone with you.

ANN. No . . . what is it, Chris, your mother?

CHRIS. No . . . nothing like that . . .

ANN. Then what's wrong? . . . Even in your letters, there was something ashamed.

CHRIS. Yes. I suppose I have been. But it's going from me.

ANN. You've got to tell me—

CHRIS. I don't know how to start. (*He takes her hand. He speaks quietly, factually at first.*)

ANN. It wouldn't work this way.[12]

(*Slight pause.*)

CHRIS. It's all mixed up with so many other things. . . . You remember, overseas, I was in command of a company?[13]

ANN. Yeah, sure.

CHRIS. Well, I lost them.

ANN. How many?

CHRIS. Just about all.

ANN. Oh, gee!

CHRIS.[14] It takes a little time to toss that off. Because they weren't just men. For instance, one time it'd been raining several days and this kid came to me, and gave me his last pair of dry socks. Put them in my pocket. That's only a little thing . . . but . . . that's the kind of guys I had. They didn't die; they killed

7. Why does he look toward the house? What is his facial expression?

8. What sort of kiss is appropriate here? Why?

9. What is the tone of Ann's voice?

10. What does Ann mean?

11. Why does Chris react like this?

12. To what is Ann referring? How does Chris react to her statement?

13. There is a change of mood. How is the transition made? What is Chris's tone of voice? What facial expressions would be appropriate?

14. In the long speech following, what positions would the two take? With what

movements,
gestures, facial
expressions does
Chris show his
feelings? What is the
tempo of the
speech? How does
Ann react while
Chris speaks?

15. What is the
purpose of the
pause?

16. How would the
tone of Chris's voice
change here?

17. What
movements does
Ann's speech
suggest? What is her
tone of voice? How
is Chris affected?

18. This off-stage
voice may be
omitted.

19. What is the
mood of this kiss?

themselves for each other. I mean that exactly; a little more selfish and they'd've been here today. And I got an idea—watching them go down. Everything was being destroyed, see, but it seemed to me that one new thing was made. A kind of . . . responsibility. Man for man. You understand me?—To show that, to bring that on to the earth again like some kind of a monument and everyone would feel it standing there, behind him, and it would make a difference to him. (*Pause.*)[15] And then I came home and it was incredible. I . . . there was no meaning in it here; the whole thing to them was a kind of a—bus accident. I went to work with Dad, and that rat-race again. I felt . . . what you said . . . ashamed somehow. Because nobody was changed at all. It seemed to make suckers out of a lot of guys. I felt wrong to be alive, to open the bank-book, to drive the new car, to see the new refrigerator. I mean you can take those things out of a war, but when you drive that car you've got to know that it came out of the love a man can have for a man, you've got to be a little better because of that. Otherwise what you have is really loot, and there's blood on it. I didn't want to take any of it.[16] And I guess that included you.

ANN. And you still feel that way?

CHRIS. I want you now, Annie.

ANN. Because you mustn't feel that way any more. Because you have a right to whatever you have. Everything, Chris, understand that? To me, too . . . And the money, there's nothing wrong in your money. Your father put hundreds of planes in the air, you should be proud. A man should be paid for that. . . .[17]

CHRIS. Oh Annie, Annie . . . I'm going to make a fortune for you!

KELLER (*offstage*).[18] Hello . . . Yes. Sure.

ANN (*laughing softly*). What'll I do with a fortune . . .? (*They kiss.*)[19]

from
ALL MY SONS
ACT 2
Arthur Miller

It is twilight, the back yard of an upper middle-class American home. There are a bench and some lawn chairs. (See page 1 for further background.)

Chris Keller has begun to suspect that his father, Joe Keller, is responsible for the manufacture and shipment of defective airplane parts used in World War II planes. As a result of the defective parts, more than twenty pilots were killed. As the following scene opens, Mrs. Keller has left Chris and his father alone in the yard after cryptically suggesting that if Chris's brother, a combat flier who has been missing in action for several years, is dead, Joe Keller is responsible.

(*Both hold their voices down.*)[1]

KELLER (*afraid of him, his deadly insistence*). What's the matter with you? What the hell is the matter with you?

CHRIS (*quietly, incredibly*). How could you do that? How?

KELLER. What's the matter with you!

CHRIS. Dad . . . Dad, you killed twenty-one men!

KELLER. What, killed?

CHRIS. You killed them, you murdered them.

KELLER (*as though throwing his whole nature open before* **CHRIS**). How could I kill anybody?

CHRIS. Dad! Dad!

KELLER (*trying to hush him*). I didn't kill anybody!

CHRIS. Then explain it to me. What did you do? Explain it to me or I'll tear you to pieces!

1. What follows is quick-moving, potentially explosive, and intimate. Detail of movement, gesture, and facial expression as well as sublety of tone are important. What, in general, is Keller's tone? Chris's tone? What are the differences in their characters? How might these be revealed physically?

KELLER (*horrified at his overwhelming fury*). Don't, Chris, don't. . . .

CHRIS. I want to know what you did, now what did you do? You had a hundred and twenty cracked engine-heads, now what did you do?

KELLER. If you're going to hang me then I . . .

CHRIS. I'm listening. God Almighty, I'm listening!

KELLER (*their movements now are those of subtle pursuit and escape.* KELLER *keeps a step out of* CHRIS' *range as he talks*).[2] You're a boy, what could I do! I'm in business, a man is in business; a hundred and twenty cracked, you're out of business; you got a process, the process don't work, you're out of business; you don't know how to operate, your stuff is no good; they close you up, they tear up your contracts, what the hell's it to them? You lay forty years into a business and they knock you out in five minutes, what could I do, let them take forty years, let them take my life away? (*His voice cracking.*) I never thought they'd install them. I swear to God. I thought they'd stop 'em before anybody took off.

CHRIS. Then why'd you ship them out?

KELLER. By the time they could spot them I thought I'd have the process going again, and I could show them they needed me and they'd let it go by. But weeks passed and I got no kick-back, so I was going to tell them.

CHRIS. Then why didn't you tell them?

KELLER. It was too late. The paper, it was all over the front page, twenty-one went down, it was too late. They came with handcuffs into the shop, what could I do? (*He sits on bench.*) Chris . . . Chris, I did it for you, it was a chance and I took it for you. I'm sixty-one years old, when would I have another chance to make something for you? Sixty-one years old you don't get another chance, do ya?[3]

CHRIS. You even knew they wouldn't hold up in the air.

KELLER. I didn't say that. . . .

CHRIS. But you were going to warn them not to use them. . . .

2. How have the preceding exchanges led to this? In what follows, when would Keller move away from Chris? When would Chris approach Keller?

3. In each of his last two speeches, Keller has given a different reason for his actions. How do his reasons differ? What do they reveal about his character? What vocal quality and manner does he use in each speech? What words would he emphasize in each speech?

KELLER. But that don't mean . . .

CHRIS. It means you knew they'd crash.

KELLER. It don't mean that.

CHRIS. Then you *thought* they'd crash.

KELLER. I was afraid maybe. . . .

CHRIS. You were afraid maybe! God in heaven, what kind of a man are you? Kids were hanging in the air by those heads.[4] You knew that!

KELLER. For you, a business for you!

CHRIS (*with burning fury*). For me! Where do you live, where have you come from? For me!—I was dying every day and you were killing my boys and you did it for me? What the hell do you think I was thinking of, the goddam business? Is that as far as your mind can see, the business? What is that, the world—the business? What the hell do you mean, you did it for me? Don't you have a country? Don't you live in the world? What the hell are you? You're not even an animal, no animal kills his own, what are you? What must I do to you? I ought to tear the tongue out of your mouth, what must I do? (*With his fist he pounds down upon his father's shoulder. He stumbles away, covering his face as he weeps.*) What must I do, Jesus God, what must I do?[5]

KELLER. Chris . . . My Chris . . .[6]

4. The cracked cylinder heads produced by Keller's company.

5. What does this speech reveal about Chris? At what point does Chris lose his anger? Why does he lose it?

6. What is the tone of Keller's voice and his physical manner?

from
DEEP ARE THE ROOTS
ACT 3
Arnaud D'Usseau and James Gow

T he Second World War has recently ended. It is winter, late at night. The
scene takes place in the large, elegant living room of Senator Langdon's
home on the outskirts of a small town in the deep South. There are a sofa,
several chairs and tables.

Lt. Charles Brett, a Negro, has recently returned from the War. In the
Army Brett had become a successful officer. At home, however, he feels that
none of the bigotry and ignorance in which he grew up has changed. Brett's
mother, Bella, is a servant in the Langdon home. Through her twenty-four
years of service Bella has earned a favored position with its degree of dignity
in the household.

Brett's return has created tension in the Langdon home. Genevra, the
Senator's twenty-year-old daughter, is romantically attracted to reticent
Brett. Alice, Genevra's older sister, however, is intimidated by traditional attitudes toward Negroes. Alice was persuaded to aid in a plot to bring false
charges of theft against Brett. Brett's arrest has killed his hopes for an en-
lightened South and destroyed his plans to become principal of a school.

In this scene Brett, after escaping his captors, has slipped into the Langdon house, where he encounters Alice alone. Bella and Howard Merrick,
Alice's fiancé, also appear later in the scene.

BRETT (*appearing from behind draperies*). No, Miss Alice, I'm not on that train! (**ALICE** *draws swiftly erect, turns to stare at him.*) Yes, they put me on the train—took me right to my seat. They told me if I ever showed my ugly face in this town again, they'd hang me. But they made a mistake. They left before the train pulled out.[1]

ALICE. What do you want?

BRETT (*with great self-control, as he backs around sofa to Right end of it, as if to cut off* **ALICE'S** *escape to the hallway*). What's the matter, Miss Alice? Can't we talk? Are you no longer my friend?

ALICE. Why did you come back here?

BRETT. You seem to be frightened. Why? You don't need to be afraid of me. I have a question to ask you. There's something I must know. Could you really make yourself believe I'm a thief? (**ALICE** *runs up Left toward bell-cord, but* **BRETT** *moves forward and stops her; she shrinks back from him a little.*) Tell me, I've got to find out. No matter what I did, couldn't you let me talk? Defend myself? Couldn't you give me a hearing?

ALICE (*hoarsely*). Get out of here.

BRETT (*moving closer to her*). Why did you do it? Why? *Why?*

ALICE (*again backing away from him, with desperate fear*). Get out of here!

BRETT (*after a moment*).[2] That's all I have to know. . . . Human beings are allowed to defend themselves—to explain—to use words. But not a "nigger." Human beings are permitted to have feelings. But not a "nigger." In your mind I'm still a slave.

ALICE. Brett, you've gone mad!

BRETT. Damn you, Alice Langdon, I would have died before I would have brought harm or suffering to Nevvy![3] Damn you, I would have cut off this arm, rather than touch her! (**ALICE** *whirls around, runs to secretary right, grabs phone.*)

ALICE (*into phone*). Operator! Operator! Get me—

BRETT (*following her quickly, he gets hold of phone, pulls it away from* **ALICE,** *rips out phone cord completely*). So

1. What is Brett's tone of voice? What would his facial expression be during his exchanges with Alice? What would be Alice's facial expressions?

2. Vary the lengths of the pauses throughout the scene. Pauses help control the tempo.

3. Genevra.

that's your answer . . . call the Sheriff . . . get me hanged. (**ALICE**, *trembling with fear, backs away from him around table right.*) All right. . . . your life against mine. Kill or be killed! (*He slowly moves quite close to her.*) **ALICE**. You beast! (*She slaps him desperately.*) **BRETT** (*seizing her by the arms, holding her motionless*). That's what they taught me . . . when I know somebody is my enemy, I can kill her. (**ALICE**, *held tightly, is motionless, paralyzed.*) No. . . . No. I don't have to kill you! You're not worth killing. Go on living. And shake with fear every time you see a black face. (*He pushes **ALICE** away from him; she staggers over Left and sinks onto coffee table in front of sofa; for a moment it looks as if she might faint. **BELLA**, passing through the hall, has heard **BRETT'S** last line and seen what is happening; she has hurried into room and seized **BRETT'S** arms, as if to restrain him from further action.*)

BELLA. Brett! Brett, son! (**BRETT** *is still regarding **ALICE** with contemptuous hatred.*) Go to my room! Stay there! Don't come out.[4]

BRETT. Look at her. White scum.

BELLA. Go to my room, you hear! (**BRETT** *goes slowly out through hallway. **BELLA** goes to buffet up Center, switches on wall-bracket lights, and pours a glass of water. she comes down to **ALICE**.*) Here, drink this water.

ALICE. I'm all right, Bella. . . . I'll be all right. You can go.

BELLA. What did you expect? An eye for an eye, a tooth for a tooth. That's in the Bible, too. . . . (*Starts toward Center, stops above **ALICE**.*) I'm sorry for you; yes, I am, young white lady in your big house. You walk a high, proud path.

ALICE. Please, Bella.

BELLA. No humbleness, no loving-kindness. . . . All right, live like that. Grow old like that. Always being the one to pass judgment, until your heart is like a rock and you've nothing left but your almighty righteousness. (*Turns to go, up Center.*)[5]

ALICE (*looking up, turns to **BELLA***) Bella— (**BELLA** *stops, up Center. **ALICE** continues in a low voice.*) Bella, you don't know what he did.[6]

4. What are Brett's and Bella's facial expressions during their confrontation?

5. How does Bella's understanding of Alice differ from Brett's? What does this reveal about their characters?

6. In the exchanges between Bella and Alice what reactions does each expect of the other? Are their expectations satisfied or disappointed? What physical manners, gestures, tones of voices will help reveal their characters?

BELLA. What he did—and what Nevvy did. Or what they did not do—

ALICE. (*helplessly*). But, Bella, it was wrong.

BELLA. Yes. But did God appoint you to cast the first stone?

ALICE. But if it was wrong—? You know it was. You know we can't let such things happen.[7]

BELLA (*crosses to* **ALICE**). Who can't let it happen? It happens. You fine and mighty white folk let it happen every day.

ALICE. What?

BELLA. At least *them* two are pure in heart. . . .[8] But this land sees real evil. Sees it all the time. Ask any black woman, young and ripe. She'll tell you about those lily-white gentlemen.

ALICE. But it's not the same.[9]

BELLA (*sits beside* **ALICE** *on coffee table*). Isn't it? Is my woman's body less sacred than yours? (*Pause.*) No, we ain't good enough to claim a place among the chosen people. But we're good enough to share the white man's bed. And when we do, God punishes us as He sees fit—but nobody calls the Sheriff.[10]

ALICE. Why, Bella—

BELLA (*rises*). Well, maybe you'll learn. We all got to accept the misery we make for ourselves, and there's plenty of it without making misery for other folks too. (**HOWARD** *enters from stairs.*)

HOWARD (*crossing to Center*). Alice, you know damn well in your heart that Brett did not take that watch. Are you willing to face that fact? Are you willing to discover the truth about yourself? Or do you still prefer to go on hugging the lie your father invented? (**ALICE** *doesn't answer.*)

BELLA. Mr. Merrick, if you can do it, I wish you'd prove the truth to her. She needs to have things proved to her. (**BELLA** *exits.*)

HOWARD. In the past you've always been very sure. Tell him you're confused.

ALICE. That's not enough.

HOWARD. But it's something. White superiority never admits confusion. (**BRETT** *enters.*) At least it's a start.

7. Which words would receive emphasis here?

8. How does Bella's view of justice differ from Alice's?

9. What vocal quality would best reflect Alice's attitudes here?

10. How might Bella's tone of voice have changed in this speech?

It's a— (*Sees* **BRETT**, *who is in arch up Center.*) Brett, come in. (**ALICE** *turns up toward* **BRETT**.)

BRETT (*to* **ALICE**, *crossing into room, up Center*). My mother told me to come in here. She said I had to listen to you.[11]

11. Would the tone of Brett's voice be different from or the same as when he exited?

ALICE (*after a moment crosses to* **BRETT**). I'm not sure that anything I can say will mean very much now. I'm not even sure I can say it properly.

BRETT. Say your piece, Miss Alice.

ALICE (*carefully, almost painfully*). There's a difference between us: Your skin is dark and my skin is white. In the world we live in today, everything conspires to make that a very great difference indeed. It's wrong, it's base, but there it is. I tried to call you my equal, I was very nice to you, but I realize now that always in my heart I felt you were different. (**BRETT** *turns away from* **ALICE**. *Frowns.*) No, that's wrong. I'll try to tell it honestly. In my heart I felt you were inferior. I hid this feeling with noble deeds; I pretended to be fair and judicious. I was even able to impress myself with my own great good-will. (*Pause.*) Well, with one blow you destroyed my lovely self-satisfaction. Whatever understanding I had, I lost in a moment. I just couldn't stop to think that you were intelligent and truthful. Like any red-necked planter, I leaped to conclusions. I invoked the white man's law. . . . I don't want to be that kind of person, Brett. I don't want hatred on my conscience. I want to be free, too. Free from fear and free from guilt. (*Aware of his un-yielding expression. Urgently.*) What can I do, Brett?[12]

12. What might be Howard's activities during Alice's speech?

BRETT. Nothing. Let me go away. Let my life be my own. That's enough. (*He starts to go, crosses up to arch* —**ALICE** *turns away hopelessly.*)

HOWARD. Lieutenant, just a moment. (*Crosses to* **BRETT**, *who stops.*) Why don't you give her a chance?

BRETT (*lashing out, turns to* **HOWARD**). A chance? What am I supposed to ask for? A check for ten thousand dollars? A written apology announcing to whomever it concerns that I'm not really a thief? No, I need no more favors.

ALICE (*turning to* **BRETT**). You're right. Favors aren't enough. I asked what I can do, because I'm not sure.

BRETT (*coldly, crossing to* **ALICE**). You'll never be sure. Wherever there are people like you, there's always a sheriff. Never sure, but always safe.

ALICE. Brett, stay in this town!

BRETT. And next time get hanged by my neck.

ALICE. Give me a chance to show you! If you'll stay here, I'll tell anyone who'll listen that it was my father who was the thief. I want to stand with you. . . . Your school, your being principal—you and I can still fight for it. . . . What do you say, Brett?

BRETT (*in a low voice*). No . . .

ALICE. You don't believe me!

BRETT. Yes, I believe you'd try to do all those things. But it's no use. We're on the opposite sides of a high wall.

ALICE. When you came back from Europe, you were ready to scale that wall. You were ready to knock it down!

BRETT. I was a fool. . . . My men were right. My boys in Italy. They weren't tricked. They knew when it comes right down to it, it's white against black—the black underneath. They weren't deceived by having an expensive education and a generous white friend. They had the satisfaction of hating—hating all white people.

HOWARD. You're suggesting that Alice may have the satisfaction of hating all Negroes.

BRETT (*defiantly*). Yes!

HOWARD. What if she doesn't want to?

BRETT. Then she can learn. There's that wall . . . I know. I've learned. Even when you've been nice to us, it's been an insult! (**ALICE** *turns up back of sofa.*) I know that now. I see that. I didn't see it before. . . . I hate you, Miss Alice, I hate all white people. (*There's a silence.*)

HOWARD (*carefully*). That's a heavy task you've set your-self—hating all white people.

BRETT. I'm not finding it so difficult.

HOWARD. That family in England. The family who entertained you in their home. On second thought, do you hate them, too?

BRETT. Yes.

HOWARD. Those Italian peasants who looked upon you as their savior—who had you sit down at their table and share a bottle of wine—you hate them, too?

BRETT. Yes. They're ignorant. But they'll learn; they'll learn I'm "inferior." There are plenty of white Americans teaching them.

HOWARD (*judiciously*). Yes, there probably are. (*Turns away from* **BRETT** *slowly, then suddenly turns back.*) Brett . . . What about Nevvy?[13] Nevvy is white. (**BRETT** *avoids looking at* **HOWARD.**) Do you hate Nevvy, too? Go on, tell me! Tell me that you hate Nevvy! (**HOWARD** *continues relentlessly.*) As long as there's one white person in the world whom you trust, you can't call us all unjust and vile. There's a—

BRETT. Shut up!

HOWARD. You admit there is one white person who is good. Then you can't declare war, because there may be others. If Nevvy—

BRETT (*furiously*). Damn you, shut up! (*Another silence.*)[14]

ALICE (*from the heart, crossing to* **HOWARD** *and* **BRETT**). Please, Brett. It's more than you and I and Nevvy. If decent people—whatever the color of their skin—can't live and work together, then there's no security in the world. There is no peace.

BRETT (*after a moment, slowly*). Then there is no peace.

13. How does Nevvy's name affect Brett? What actions and/or facial expressions would reveal this?

14. What happens both on stage and within each character during this silence?

from
AH, WILDERNESS!
ACT 4, SCENE 2
Eugene O'Neill

It is nine o'clock on a warm July evening, 1906. The scene is set in the vicinity of a rowboat on a strip of beach along the harbor of a small town in Connecticut.

Richard Miller, seventeen years old, is in trouble with his parents for sending love poems to his girl friend, Muriel, who is fifteen. Muriel's parents believe the poems are vulgar. Though forbidden to meet, Richard and Muriel have arranged an evening rendezvous. When this scene begins, Muriel is late for her date with Richard. As he waits for her, Richard recalls his visit to a disreputable roadhouse the night before and his encounter there with an aggressive prostitute.

(**RICHARD** *is discovered sitting sideways on the gunwale of the rowboat near the stern. He is facing left, watching the path. He is in a great state of anxious expectancy, squirming about uncomfortably on the narrow gunwale, kicking at the sand restlessly, twirling his straw hat, with a bright-colored band in stripes, around on his finger.*)

RICHARD (*thinking aloud*).[1] Must be nearly nine. . . . I can hear the Town Hall clock strike, it's so still tonight . . . Gee, I'll bet Ma had a fit when she found out I'd sneaked out . . . I'll catch hell when I get back, but it'll be worth it . . . if only Muriel turns up . . . she didn't say for certain she could . . . gosh, I wish she'd come! . . . am I sure she wrote nine? . . . (*He puts the straw hat on the seat amidships and pulls the folded letter out of his pocket and peers at it in the moonlight.*) Yes, it's nine, all right. (*He starts to put the note back in his pocket, then stops and kisses it — then shoves it*

1. A long speech follows. Richard is alone on the stage. The actor's movements and the changes in his voice will help keep the audience's attention and show Richard's changes of mood. At what points would the tone of Richard's voice change? Study the character to develop an appropriate pattern of gesture and movement to show his changes in thought.

away hastily, sheepish, looking around him shamefacedly, as if afraid he were being observed.) Aw, that's silly . . . no, it isn't either . . . not when you're really in love. . . . (*He jumps to his feet restlessly.*) Darn it, I wish she'd show up! . . . think of something else . . . that'll make the time pass quicker . . . where was I this time last night? . . . waiting outside the Pleasant Beach House . . . Belle . . . ah, forget her! . . . now, when Muriel's coming . . . that's a fine time to think of−! . . . but you hugged and kissed her . . . not until I was drunk, I didn't . . . and then it was all showing off . . . darned fool! . . . and I didn't go upstairs with her . . . even if she was pretty . . . aw, she wasn't pretty . . . she was all painted up . . . she was just a whore . . . she was everything dirty . . . Muriel's a million times prettier anyway . . . Muriel and I will go upstairs . . . when we're married . . . but that will be beautiful . . . but I oughtn't even to think of that yet . . . it's not right . . . I'd never− now . . . and she'd never . . . she's a decent girl . . . I couldn't love her if she wasn't . . . but after we're married. . . . (*He gives a little shiver of passionate longing−then resolutely turns his mind away from these improper, almost desecrating thoughts.*) That damned barkeep kicking me . . . I'll bet you if I hadn't been drunk I'd have given him one good punch in the nose, even if he could have licked me after! . . . (*Then with a shiver of shamefaced revulsion and self-disgust.*) Aw, you deserved a kick in the pants . . . making such a darned slob of yourself . . . reciting the Ballad of Reading Gaol to those lowbrows! . . . you must have been a fine sight when you got home! . . . having to be put to bed and getting sick! . . . Phaw! . . . (*He squirms disgustedly.*) Think of something else, can't you? . . . recite something . . . see if you remember . . .

"Nay, let us walk from the fire unto fire
From passionate pain to deadlier delight−
I am too young to live without desire,
Too young art thou to waste this summernight−"

. gee, that's a peach! . . . I'll have to memorize the rest and recite it to Muriel the next time. . . . I wish I could write poetry . . . about her and me. . . . (*He sighs and stares around him at the night.*) Gee, it's beautiful tonight . . . as if it was a special night . . . for me and Muriel. . . . Gee, I love tonight. . . . I love the sand, and the trees, and the grass, and the water and the sky, and the moon . . . it's all in me and I'm in it . . . God, it's so beautiful! (*He stands staring at the moon with a rapt face. From the distance the Town Hall clock begins to strike. This brings him back to earth with a start.*) There's nine now. . . . (*He peers at the path apprehensively.*) I don't see her . . . she must have got caught. . . . (*Almost tearfully.*) Gee, I hate to go home and catch hell . . . without having seen her! . . . (*Then calling a manly cynicism to his aid.*) Aw, who ever heard of a woman ever being on time. . . . I ought to know enough about life by this time not to expect . . . (*Then with sudden excitement.*) There she comes now. . . . Gosh! (*He heaves a huge sigh of relief — then recites dramatically to himself, his eyes on the approaching figure.*)

"And lo my love, mine own soul's heart, more dear
Than mine own soul, more beautiful than God,
Who hath my being between the hands of her — "

(*Then hastily.*) Mustn't let her know I'm so tickled. . . . I ought to be mad about that first letter, anyway . . . if women are too sure of you, they treat you like slaves . . . let her suffer, for a change. . . . (*He starts to stroll around with exaggerated carelessness, turning his back on the path, hands in pockets, whistling with insouciance "Waiting at the Church."* MURIEL MC COMBER *enters from down the path, Left front. She is fifteen, going on sixteen. She is a pretty girl with a plump, graceful little figure, fluffy, light-brown hair, big naïve wondering dark eyes, a round, dimpled face, a melting drawly voice. Just now she is in a great thrilled state of mind of timid adventurousness. She hesitates in the shadow at the foot of the path, waiting for* RICHARD *to see her; but he resolutely goes on whistling with back turned, and she has to*

2. In the exchanges between Richard and Muriel, when is each revealing true feelings? When does each hide true feelings? What changes in gestures, rate of speech, vocal tone, and movement will help reveal the characters' real attitudes?

call him.)[2]

MURIEL. Oh, Dick.

RICHARD (*turns around with an elaborate simulation of being disturbed in the midst of profound meditation*). Oh, hello. Is it nine already? Gosh, time passes—when you're thinking.

MURIEL (*coming toward him as far as the edge of the shadow—disappointedly*). I thought you'd be waiting right here at the end of the path. I'll bet you'd forgotten I was even coming.

RICHARD (*strolling a little toward her but not too far—carelessly*). No, I hadn't forgotten, honest. But I got to thinking about life.

MURIEL. You might think of me for a change, after all the risk I've run to see you! (*Hesitating timidly on the edge of the shadow.*) Dick! You come here to me. I'm afraid to go out in that bright moonlight where anyone might see me.

RICHARD (*coming toward her—scornfully*). Aw, there you go again—always scared of life!

MURIEL (*indignantly*). Dick Miller, I do think you've got an awful nerve to say that after all the risks I've run making this date and then sneaking out! You didn't take the trouble to sneak any letter to me, I notice!

RICHARD. No, because after your first letter, I thought everything was dead and past between us.

MURIEL. And I'll bet you didn't care one little bit! (*On the verge of humiliated tears.*) Oh, I was a fool ever to come here! I've got a good notion to go right home and never speak to you again! (*She half turns back toward the path.*)

RICHARD (*frightened—immediately becomes terribly sincere—grabbing her hand*). Aw, don't go, Muriel! Please! I didn't mean anything like that, honest I didn't! Gee, if you knew how broken-hearted I was by that first letter, and how darned happy your second letter made me—!

MURIEL (*happily relieved—but appreciates she has the upper hand now and doesn't relent at once*). I don't believe you.

3. Richard's sister, Mildred.

RICHARD. You ask Mid[3] how happy I was. She can

prove it.

MURIEL. She'd say anything you told her to. I don't care anything about what she'd say. It's you. You've got to swear to me —

RICHARD. I swear!

MURIEL (*demurely*). Well then, all right, I'll believe you.

RICHARD (*his eyes on her face lovingly — genuine adoration in his voice*). Gosh, you're pretty tonight, Muriel! It seems ages since we've been together! If you knew how I've suffered — !

MURIEL. I did, too.

RICHARD (*unable to resist falling into his tragic literary pose for a moment*). The despair in my soul — (*He recites dramatically.*) "Something was dead in each of us, And what was dead was Hope!" That was me! My hope of happiness was dead! (*Then with sincere boyish fervor.*) Gosh, Muriel, it sure is wonderful to be with you again! (*He puts a timid arm around her awkwardly.*)

MURIEL (*shyly*). I'm glad — it makes you happy. I'm happy, too.

RICHARD. Can't I — won't you let me kiss you now? Please! (*He bends his face toward hers.*)

MURIEL (*ducking her head away — timidly*) No. You mustn't. Don't —

RICHARD. Aw, why can't I?

MURIEL. Because — I'm afraid.

RICHARD (*discomfited — taking his arm from around her — a bit sulky and impatient with her*). Aw, that's what you always say! You're always so afraid! Aren't you ever going to let me?

MURIEL. I will — sometime.

RICHARD. When?

MURIEL. Soon, maybe.

RICHARD. Tonight, will you?

MURIEL (*coyly*). I'll see.

RICHARD. Promise?

MURIEL. I promise — maybe.

RICHARD. All right. You remember you've promised. (*Then coaxingly.*) Aw, don't let's stand here. Come on out and we can sit down in the boat.

MURIEL (*hesitantly*). It's so bright out there.

RICHARD. No one'll see. You know there's never any-one around here at night.

MURIEL (*illogically*). I know there isn't. That's why I thought it would be the best place. But there might be someone.

RICHARD (*taking her hand and tugging at it gently*). There isn't a soul. (MURIEL *steps out a little and looks up and down fearfully.* RICHARD *goes on insistently.*) Aw, what's the use of a moon if you can't see it!

MURIEL. But it's only a new moon. That's not much to look at.

RICHARD. But I want to see you. I can't here in the shadow. I want to —drink in—all your beauty.

MURIEL (*can't resist this*). Well, all right—only I can't stay only a few minutes. (*She lets him lead her toward the stern of the boat.*)

RICHARD (*pleadingly*). Aw, you can stay a little while, can't you? Please! (*He helps her in and she settles herself in the stern seat of the boat, facing diagonally left front.*)

MURIEL. A little while. (*He sits beside her.*) But I've got to be home in bed again pretending to be asleep by ten o'clock. That's the time Pa and Ma come up to bed, as regular as clock work, and Ma always looks into my room.

RICHARD. But you have oodles of time to do that.

MURIEL (*excitedly*). Dick, you have no idea what I went through to get here tonight! My, but it was exciting! You know Pa's punishing me by sending me to bed at eight sharp, and I had to get all undressed and into bed 'cause at half-past he sends Ma up to make sure I've obeyed, and she came up, and I pretended to be asleep, and she went down again, and I got up and dressed in such a hurry—I must look a sight, don't I?

RICHARD. You do not! You look wonderful!

MURIEL. And then I sneaked down the back stairs. And the pesky old stairs squeaked, and my heart was in my mouth, I was so scared, and then I sneaked out through the back yard, keeping in the dark under the trees, and—My, but it was exciting! Dick, you don't realize how I've been punished for your sake. Pa's been so mean and nasty, I've almost hated him![4]

RICHARD. And you don't realize what I've been through for you—and what I'm in for—for sneaking out—(*Then darkly.*) And for what I did last night—what your letter made me do!

MURIEL (*made terribly curious by his ominous tone*). What did my letter make you do?

RICHARD (*beginning to glory in this*). It's too long a story—and let the dead past bury its dead. (*Then with real feeling.*) Only it isn't past, I can tell you! What I'll catch when Pa gets hold of me!

MURIEL. Tell me, Dick! Begin at the beginning and tell me!

RICHARD (*tragically*). Well, after your old—your father left our place I caught holy hell from Pa.

MURIEL. You mustn't swear!

RICHARD (*somberly*). Hell is the only word that can describe it. And on top of that, to torture me more, he gave me your letter. After I'd read that I didn't want to live any more. Life seemed like a tragic farce.

MURIEL. I'm so awful sorry, Dick—honest I am! But you might have known I'd never write that unless—

RICHARD. I thought your love for me was dead. I thought you'd never loved me, that you'd only been cruelly mocking me—to torture me!

MURIEL. Dick! I'd never! You know I'd never!

RICHARD. I wanted to die. I sat and brooded about death. Finally I made up my mind I'd kill myself.

MURIEL (*excitedly*). Dick! You didn't!

RICHARD. I did, too! If there'd been one of Hedda Gabler's[5] pistols around, you'd have seen if I wouldn't have done it beautifully! I thought, when I'm dead, she'll be sorry she ruined my life.

MURIEL (*cuddling up a little to him*). If you ever had! I'd have died, too! Honest, I would!

RICHARD. But suicide is the act of a coward. That's what stopped me. (*Then with a bitter change of tone.*) And anyway, I thought to myself, she isn't worth it.

MURIEL (*huffily*). That's a nice thing to say!

4. How would Muriel dramatize her escape? Which words would be emphasized?

5. A character in a play by Henrik Ibsen.

RICHARD. Well, if you meant what was in that letter, you wouldn't have been worth it, would you?

MURIEL. But I've told you Pa—

RICHARD. So I said to myself, I'm through with women; they're all alike!

MURIEL. I'm not.

RICHARD. And I thought, what difference does it make what I do now? I might as well forget her and lead the pace that kills, and drown my sorrows! You know I had eleven dollars saved up to buy you something for your birthday, but I thought, she's dead to me now and why shouldn't I throw it away? (*Then hastily.*) I've still got almost five left, Muriel, and I can get you something nice with that.

MURIEL (*excitedly*). What do I care about your old presents? You tell me what you did!

RICHARD (*darkly again*). After it was dark, I sneaked out and went to a low dive I know about.

MURIEL. Dick Miller, I don't believe you ever!

RICHARD. You ask them at the Pleasant Beach House if I didn't! They won't forget me in a hurry!

6. How might this be shown?

MURIEL (*impressed and horrified*).[6] You went there? Why, that's a terrible place! Pa says it ought to be closed by the police!

7. What vocal qualities and/or movements make Richard's speech dark?

RICHARD (*darkly*).[7] I said it was a dive, didn't I? It's a "secret house of shame." And they let me into a secret room behind the barroom. There wasn't anyone there but a Princeton Senior I know—he belongs to Tiger Inn and he's fullback on the football team—and he had two chorus girls from New York with him, and they were all drinking champagne.

MURIEL (*disturbed by the entrance of the chorus girls*). Dick Miller! I hope you didn't notice—

RICHARD (*carelessly*). I had a high-ball by myself and then I noticed one of the girls—the one that wasn't with the fullback—looking at me. She had strange-looking eyes. And then she asked me if I wouldn't drink champagne with them and come and sit with her.

MURIEL. She must have been a nice thing! (*Then a bit falteringly.*) And did—you?

RICHARD (*with tragic bitterness*). Why shouldn't I, when you'd told me in that letter you'd never see me again?

MURIEL (*almost tearfully*). But you ought to have known Pa made me—

RICHARD. I didn't know that then. (*Then rubbing it in.*) Her name was Belle. She had yellow hair—the kind that burns and stings you!

MURIEL. I'll bet it was dyed!

RICHARD. She kept smoking one cigarette after another —but that's nothing for a chorus girl.

MURIEL (*indignantly*). She was low and bad, that's what she was or she couldn't be a chorus girl, and her smoking cigarettes proves it! (*Then falteringly again.*) And then what happened?

RICHARD (*carelessly*).[8] Oh, we just kept drinking champagne—I bought a round—and then I had a fight with the barkeep and knocked him down because he'd insulted her. He was a great big thug but—

MURIEL (*huffily*). I don't see how he could—insult that kind! And why did you fight for her? Why didn't the Princeton fullback who'd brought them there? He must have been bigger than you.

RICHARD (*stopped for a moment—then quickly*). He was too drunk by that time.

MURIEL. And were you drunk?

RICHARD. Only a little then. I was worse later. (*Proudly*) You ought to have seen me when I got home! I was on the verge of delirium tremens!

MURIEL. I'm glad I didn't see you. You must have been awful. I hate people who get drunk. I'd have hated you!

RICHARD. Well, it was all your fault, wasn't it? If you hadn't written that letter—

MURIEL. But I've told you I didn't mean—(*Then faltering but fascinated.*) But what happened with that Belle—after—before you went home?

RICHARD. Oh, we kept drinking champagne and she said she'd fallen in love with me at first sight and she came and sat on my lap and kissed me.

MURIEL (*stiffening*). Oh!

RICHARD (*quickly, afraid he has gone too far*). But it was

8. In the following speeches, Richard uses a variety of vocal tones. What gestures, facial expressions, and movements might be appropriate to them?

only all in fun, and then we just kept on drinking champagne, and finally I said good night and came home.

MURIEL. And did you kiss her?

RICHARD. No, I didn't.

MURIEL (*distractedly*). You did, too! You're lying and you know it. You did, too! (*Then tearfully.*) And there I was right at that time lying in bed not able to sleep, wondering how I was ever going to see you again and crying my eyes out, while you——! (*She suddenly jumps to her feet in a tearful fury.*) I hate you! I wish you were dead! I'm going home this minute! I never want to lay eyes on you again! And this time I mean it! (*She tries to jump out of the boat but he holds her back. All the pose has dropped from him now and he is in a frightened state of contrition.*)

RICHARD (*imploringly*). Muriel! Wait! Listen!

MURIEL. I don't want to listen! Let me go! If you don't I'll bite your hand!

RICHARD. I won't let you go! You've got to let me explain! I never—! Ouch! (*For* MURIEL *has bitten his hand and it hurts, and, stung by the pain, he lets go instinctively, and she jumps quickly out of the boat and starts running toward the path.* RICHARD *calls after her with bitter despair and hurt.*) All right! Go if you want to—if you haven't the decency to let me explain! I hate you, too! I'll go and see Belle!

from
THE CHALK GARDEN
ACT 1
Enid Bagnold

I t is a cool afternoon in mid-June. This scene takes place in a room of a manor house in a village in Sussex, near the sea. Through the French windows one can see a garden.

Madrigal, having served a prison term, is applying for a job of governess. She is in her late forties. Laurel, the sixteen-year-old girl for whom Madrigal will care, lives with her grandmother. In this scene Madrigal and Laurel are alone for the first time.

LAUREL (*with interest*). Are you a hospital nurse?

MADRIGAL. Why do you ask?

LAUREL. You have that unmeaning way of saying things.

MADRIGAL (*after a second's pause and with a little formal manner of adapting herself*). Now that we are alone am I to call you Laurel?

LAUREL (*moves downstage on sofa*). It's my name.

MADRIGAL (*sitting beside her*).[1] And what are you interested in, Laurel? I mean—apart from yourself?

1. How would Laurel respond to this action?

LAUREL. What I don't like—is to be questioned.

MADRIGAL. I agree with you.

LAUREL. But I don't like to be agreed with—just in case I might argue! And I don't like to be read aloud to unless I suggest it! But if read aloud to—*I don't like emphasis!* And every morning I don't like *"Good morning"* said! I can see for myself what sort of day it is!

MADRIGAL. You sound as if you had lady-companions before. How did you get rid of them?

2. An old manservant.

LAUREL. I tell Pinkbell.[2]

MADRIGAL. He tells your grandmother. My mind works more slowly than yours. But it was going that way.

LAUREL. You see she loves to advertise! She loves what comes out of it. It's like dredging in the sea, she says—so much comes up in the net!

MADRIGAL. I—for instance?

LAUREL. Why not?

MADRIGAL. Doesn't she take a chance—that way?

LAUREL. No, she says you get more out of life by *hap*hazard. By the way, if you want to get on with my grandmother—you must notice her eccentricity.

MADRIGAL. She is fond of that?

LAUREL. She adores it! Oh, the tales I let her tell me when I am in the mood!

MADRIGAL (*Pause*). Does she love you?

3. What movement, gesture, tone of voice would be appropriate?

LAUREL. She would like to! (*Confidentially.*)[3] She thinks she does!—But I am only her remorse.

MADRIGAL. You try your foot upon the ice, don't you?

LAUREL. I find you wonderfully odd. Why do you come here?

4. What change has taken place in the interview?

MADRIGAL. I have to do something with my life—[4]

LAUREL. What life have you been used to?

MADRIGAL (*softly*). Regularity. Punctuality. Early rising—

LAUREL. It sounds like a prison!

MADRIGAL.—and what are *you* used to?

5. In what manner does Laurel answer? What is the tone of her question?

LAUREL. Doing what I like. (*Rises behind sofa.*) Have you been told *why* I am peculiar?[5]

MADRIGAL. Something was said about it.

LAUREL. If you come here we'll talk for hours and hours about it! I'll tell you everything! And why I hate my mother!

MADRIGAL. I too hated my mother. I should say it was my stepmother.

LAUREL. Oh, that's just an ordinary hatred. Mine is more special.[6]

MADRIGAL. The dangerous thing about hate is that it seems so reasonable.

LAUREL. Maitland won't let me say so, but my mother is Jezebel! She is so overloaded with sex that it sparkles! She is golden and striped — like something in the jungle!

MADRIGAL. You sound proud of her. Does she never come here?

LAUREL (*below armchair*). To see me? Never! She's too busy with love! Just now she's in Arabia with her para*mour*! (*Sits.*)

MADRIGAL. With her — ?

LAUREL. If you pin me down he is my stepfather! Have you read Hamlet? It tipped my mind and turned me against my mother.

MADRIGAL. Does she know you feel discarded?

LAUREL. I don't. I left her! (*Pause.*) The night before she married — she forgot to say goodnight to me — Does that sound a very little thing?

MADRIGAL (*with sudden passion*). Oh no! It lights up everything.

LAUREL (*looking at her*). Are you talking of you? Or of me![7]

MADRIGAL (*her hand on her breast*). When one feels wrongly — it is always of me!

LAUREL. Oh, if you are not a spy sent by my grandmother, I shall enjoy you! Do you know about crime? Maitland and I share a crime library. Bit by bit we are collecting the Notable Trial Series.

MADRIGAL (*low*). Don't you like detective stories better?

LAUREL. No, we like real murder! The trials. We act the parts.

MADRIGAL (*faintly*). Which — trials have you got?

LAUREL. So far — only Mrs. Maybrick, Lizzie Borden,

6. In her next speeches Laurel reveals the special quality of her hatred. What is it? What does it reveal about her character? What tone of voice and gestures will help reveal this?

7. What is the tone of Laurel's voice?

Dr. Crippen. But Maitland likes the murder*esses* better. He's half in love with them. Oh, if you come here—

MADRIGAL. Here!—(*Rises with gloves and handbag. Comes Left Center.*)

LAUREL.—couldn't we act them together? (*Gets no answer.*) Maitland is so slow I make him read the prisoner. (*Rises. Passes below her to Below Left chairs.*) Why does the prisoner have so little to say? (*Waits.*) —do you think? (*Pause—no answer.*)[8] What a habit you have—haven't you—of not answering.

MADRIGAL. I made an answer.

LAUREL. Only to yourself, I think.[9]

8. What has this scene revealed about the characters? What relationship has begun between them?

9. What does Laurel mean?

Courtesy of the American Conservatory Theatre. **The Chalk Garden** (l to r) Miss Madrigal (Barbara Dirickson) and Laurel (Annette Bening).

Courtesy of the American Conservatory Theatre. **The Chalk Garden** (l to r) Laurel (Annette Bening) and Miss Madrigal (Barbara Dirickson).

from
THE CHALK GARDEN
ACT 1
Enid Bagnold

It is an afternoon in mid-June. The action is set in a room of a manor house in a village in Sussex, near the sea. French windows open into a garden. (See page 25 for further background).

Mrs. St. Maugham is a strong-willed old woman who was once a beautiful hostess to London society. She tries to avoid a sense of old age by raising her granddaughter, Laurel, and by growing flowers. Her garden, however, is chaotic and her granddaughter is rebellious. She is guided and abetted in her futile gardening by her ancient manservant, Pinkbell, who is dying in an upstairs bedroom. Although he never appears, Pinkbell's influence is felt throughout the play.

In this scene Olivia, who is Mrs. St. Maugham's daughter and Laurel's mother, has returned after a long absence. She has remarried and is expecting another child. She now wants Laurel to come live with her. Appearing at the end of the scene is Madrigal, who is considering a job as Laurel's governess. An actress playing Madrigal should be familiar with the preceding scene in this book.

(MRS. ST. MAUGHAM *enters.*)

MRS. ST. MAUGHAM. Olivia! So soon! But you're safe—that's all that matters!

OLIVIA. Mother!—(*They embrace.*)

MRS. ST. MAUGHAM. Oh let me look at you! How brown you are! You look like an Arab. (*Brings her down stage.*) How is the desert, darling? I can almost see the sand in your hair. (OLIVIA *sits armchair.* MRS. ST. MAUGHAM *on sofa.*)

OLIVIA. Mother—how's the child?

MRS. ST. MAUGHAM (*stung*). Ask for *me*—ask for *me*, Olivia!

OLIVIA. I do, I would, but you ran in like a girl, and not a day older. As I came in—the standards dripping with roses. Oh the English flowers after the East!

MRS. ST. MAUGHAM. Let me tell you before we talk—

OLIVIA. —before we quarrel![1]

MRS. ST. MAUGHAM. No—not this time! I was going to say—that I've missed you. If I'd known you were coming I'd have driven up to see you. Whatever—and in your condition—made you rush down here without a word!

OLIVIA. I flew. I got here this morning.

MRS. ST. MAUGHAM. Like one of those crickets that leap from a distance and fall at one's feet! How do you do it?

OLIVIA (*gloves off*). By breakfasting in Baghdad and dining in Kuffra and taking a taxi in England. We're on a course. I wrote. Two months at Aldershot.

MRS. ST. MAUGHAM. Aldershot! Oh—who would have thought you would have taken on that look—so quickly—of a Colonel's Lady! What is it they call it—Reveille? How are the bugles at dawn, Olivia?

OLIVIA. We don't live in a camp.

MRS. ST. MAUGHAM. I feel sure you said you did!

OLIVIA. Never mind the camp. I want to talk to you.

MRS. ST. MAUGHAM. But why down here the very second that you arrive—and without warning!

OLIVIA. Mother, I've come about Laurel—don't put me off any longer.

MRS. ST. MAUGHAM (*to distract from main issue*). Did you

1. The women actually do quarrel. Study the progress of the quarrel. When does it begin and climax? What gestures, movements, facial expressions at specific points will help dramatize the conflicts between mother and daughter? When would they be physically close, when apart?

wear that scarf—on purpose to annoy me! What you wear is a language to me!

OLIVIA (*indignant*). That's an old battle—and an old method!

MRS. ST. MAUGHAM. When I've *told* you—in letter after letter.

OLIVIA. It's time I saw for myself, Mother! For nine years I shut the world out for her—

MRS. ST. MAUGHAM (*rises*). Nine years of widowhood might have been spent better! (*Above chair to Left of it.*) I asked you *not* to come—but you *come*! I asked you to warn me—but you ignore it! And how can you wear beige with your skin that color!

OLIVIA. Does it never become possible to talk as one grown woman to another!

MRS. ST. MAUGHAM. The gap's lessening! After fifty I haven't grown much wiser! (*Turns Up Center.*)—but at least I know what the world has to have—though one cannot pass anything on! When I count my ambitions and what you have made of them!

OLIVIA. I did what you wanted—!

MRS. ST. MAUGHAM. But *how* you resisted me! I was burning for you to cut ice in the world—yet you had to be *driven* out to gaiety! I had to beat you into beauty! You had to be lit—as one lights a lantern! Decked—like a May-tree—

OLIVIA. Oh, can't we be three minutes together—

MRS. ST. MAUGHAM (*down stage again*). Even your wedding dress you wore like wrapping paper! And where is it now—the success to which I pushed you? Laurel might have been a child, these four years, playing in a high walled park—(*Sits upper chair Left.*)

OLIVIA. —and I might have been a widow, with deer gazing at me! But life isn't like that! You had for me the standards of another age. The standards of—Pinkbell.

MRS. ST. MAUGHAM. Shy, plain, obstinate, silent. But I won. I married you.

OLIVIA (*rises. To her*). But you won't meet the man *I* married—the man *I* love!

MRS. ST. MAUGHAM. Love can be had any day! Success

is far harder.

OLIVIA. You say that off the top of your head—where you wore your tiara!

MRS. ST. MAUGHAM. So you have found a tongue to speak with![2]

OLIVIA. I have found many things—and learned others. I have been warmed and praised and made to speak. Things come late to me. Love came late to me. Laurel was born in a kind of strange virginity. To have a child doesn't always make a mother. And you won't give up the image of me! Coltish—inept, dropping the china—picking up the pieces—

MRS. ST. MAUGHAM. It was I who picked up the pieces, Olivia.

OLIVIA (*passionately*). I know. But I'm without her.

MRS. ST. MAUGHAM. You are going to have another child!

OLIVIA. This child's the Unknown! Laurel's my daughter!

MRS. ST. MAUGHAM. Who came to me—? (*Rises.*) Who ran to me—as an asylum from her mother! (*Crosses below her to armchair.*)

OLIVIA (*desperately*). Oh—you find such words to change things! You talk as if I were a light woman!

MRS. ST. MAUGHAM (*sits*). No, you are not light. You have never been a light woman. You are a dark, a mute woman. If there was lightness in you it was I who lent it to you! And all that I did—gone![3]

OLIVIA (*steps to her*). Mother! Of a thousand thousand rows between you and me—and this not, I know, the last one—be on my side! Oh—for once be on my side! Help me.

MRS. ST. MAUGHAM. To what?

OLIVIA. Help me to find her! Help me to take her back!

MRS. ST. MAUGHAM. Take her back! (*Lighting on an idea.*) What, now?—Just now! When I've found such a companion for her! A woman of the highest character! Of vast experience! I have put myself out endlessly to find her![4]

OLIVIA. She can help you to prepare her. When I come

2. In what ways has Olivia's manner changed from the beginning of the scene?

3. What does Olivia mean by "light?" What does Mrs. St. Maugham mean by it?

4. What is Mrs. St. Maugham trying to do at this point? How is it consistent with her character?

back for her—

MRS. ST. MAUGHAM. You mean before the baby's born? That will be an odd moment—won't it—to come for her!

OLIVIA (*passionately*). No! It's *why* I want her! Before I love the baby! (*Crossing to sofa.*) I can't sleep! I can't rest. I seem to myself to have abandoned her! (*Sits. Faces down stage.*)

MRS. ST. MAUGHAM. To her own grandmother! I am not a baby-farmer or a head-mistress or the matron of an orphanage—

OLIVIA (*turns on sofa*). But she'll be a woman! And I'll never have known her!

MRS. ST. MAUGHAM. It suited you when you first married that I should have her. Laurel came to me of her own free will and I have turned my old age into a nursery for her.

OLIVIA (*with indignation*). And God has given you a second chance to be a mother!

MRS. ST. MAUGHAM (*rises*). Olivia!—Oh, there is no one who puts me in a passion like you do! (*Crossing over to Left chairs with indignation.*)

OLIVIA (*rises*). And no one who knows you so well. And knows today is hopeless—

MADRIGAL (*enters from the garden up Center on a high wave of indignation—matching the crescendo of the other two. Menacing—accusing—pulling on a glove*). Mrs. St. Maugham—there must be some *mistake!* This is a chalk garden! Who has tried to grow rhododendrons in a *chalk garden?*[5]

MRS. ST. MAUGHAM (*taken aback*). Rhododendrons? We put them in last autumn. But they're unhappy! (*Sits. Picks up catalogue.*)

MADRIGAL (*magnificent, stern*). They are *dying.* They are in pure lime. Not so much as a little leaf-mould! There is no evidence of palliation! (*To upstage table for bag.*)

MRS. ST. MAUGHAM. Wait—wait—Where are you going?

MADRIGAL (*over her shoulder—going*). They could have had compost! But the compost-heap is stone-cold!

5. How does Madrigal's entrance change the situation? Timing of action is important here.

6. What might Olivia be doing while Madrigal and Mrs. St. Maugham speak?

7. What relationships between the three characters are suggested in what follows? What facial expressions will help reveal them?

8. What is the tone of Madrigal's voice?

Nothing in the world has been done for them.[6]
(*A gay* SCREAM *is heard from the garden.*)[7]

OLIVIA (*to up Right. Looks towards garden. To* MADRIGAL). Is that Laurel? She's screaming. What's the matter?

MADRIGAL (*scornful*). There is nothing the matter! She is dancing around the bonfire with the manservant.

MRS. ST. MAUGHAM. I should have told you—this is Miss Madrigal. (*Opening catalogue.*) Not so fast! I want to ask you—the bergamot—and the gunnera—

(OLIVIA *takes handbag from up stage table.*)

MADRIGAL. —won't thrive on chalk. (*Turns away to first step.*)[8]

MRS. ST. MAUGHAM. There's an east slope I can grow nothing on.

MADRIGAL. —the soil can't give what it has not got. (*On to second step.*)

OLIVIA (*crossing to her*). Don't go! The wind blows from the sea here and growing things need protection!

MADRIGAL (*suddenly halted by the look on* OLIVIA'S *face*). —and the lilies have rust—there is blackspot on the roses—and the child is screaming in the garden. . . .

MRS. ST. MAUGHAM. The roses! What would you have done for them. Pinkbell ordered—and I sprayed them!

MADRIGAL (*magnificent, contemptuous*.). With *what*, I wonder! You had better have prayed for them! (*They measure each other for a moment.*) If you will accept me—(*Goes right up to her.*) I will *take* this situation, Mrs. St. Maugham.

(OLIVIA *quietly exits.*)

(*With a dry lightness.*) You have been very badly advised—I think—by Mr. Pinkbell.

from
THE LITTLE FOXES
ACT 3
Lillian Hellman

It is spring of 1900. The action takes place in the large, expensively furnished living room of the Giddens house in a small town in the South.
There is a sweeping circular staircase leading to a second floor.

Horace Giddens is a wealthy banker who has recently been discharged from
the hospital and is under treatment for a heart ailment. He is in a wheelchair. During his absence Giddens' attractive and self-seeking wife, Regina,
and her brothers, Ben and Oscar, became involved in a potentially lucrative
financial scheme. The three have counted on using Giddens' money to com-
plete their dealing. Giddens, however, refuses to loan them the funds. Unknown to Regina, her brothers steal some negotiable bonds from Giddens'
safe-deposit box, thereby cutting her out of the deal. In the following scene
Giddens has just learned of the theft. He hears Regina enter and quickly
decides to confront her.

(**HORACE'S** *chair is now so placed that he is in front of the*
table with the medicine. **REGINA** *stands in the hall, shakes*
umbrella, stands it in the corner, takes off her cloak and
throws it over the banister. She stares at **HORACE.**)
REGINA (*as she takes off her gloves*). We had agreed that
you were to stay in your part of this house and I in
mine. This room is *my* part of the house. Please don't
come down here again.
HORACE. I won't.
REGINA (*crosses towards bell-cord*). I'll get Cal to take you
upstairs.
HORACE (*smiles*). Before you do I want to tell you that

after all, we have invested our money in Hubbard Sons and Marshall, Cotton Manufacturers.

REGINA (*stops, turns, stares at him*). What are you talking about? You haven't seen Ben—When did you change your mind?

HORACE. I didn't change my mind. I didn't invest the money. (*Smiles.*)[1] It was invested for me.

REGINA (*angrily*). What—?

HORACE. I had eighty-eight thousand dollars' worth of Union Pacific bonds in that safe-deposit box. They are not there now. Go and look. (*As she stares at him, he points to the box.*) Go and look, Regina. (*She crosses quickly to the box, opens it.*) Those bonds are as negotiable as money.

REGINA (*turns back to him*). What kind of joke are you playing now? Is this for my benefit?[2]

HORACE. I don't look in that box very often, but three days ago, on Wednesday it was, because I had made a decision—[3]

REGINA. I want to know what you are talking about.

HORACE (*sharply*). Don't interrupt me again. Because I had made a decision, I sent for the box. The bonds were gone. Eighty-eight thousand dollars gone. (*He smiles at her.*)

REGINA (*after a moment's silence, quietly*). Do you think I'm crazy enough to believe what you're saying?[4]

HORACE (*shrugs*). Believe anything you like.

REGINA (*stares at him, slowly*). Where did they go to?

HORACE. They are in Chicago. With Mr. Marshall, I should guess.

REGINA. What did they do? Walk to Chicago? Have you really gone crazy?[5]

HORACE. Leo took the bonds.

REGINA (*turns sharply, then speaks softly, without conviction*). I don't believe it.

HORACE (*leans forward*). I wasn't there but I can guess what happened. This fine gentleman, to whom you were willing to marry your daughter, took the keys and opened the box. You remember that the day of the fight Oscar went to Chicago? Well, he went with my bonds that his son Leo had stolen for him. (*Pleas-*

1. What is the nature of Horace's smile?

2. What is Regina's manner and the tone of her voice?

3. How would Horace's rate of speech differ from Regina's?

4. What might go on between Horace and Regina during the pause?

5. What is the tone of Regina's voice?

antly.) And for Ben, of course, too.[6]

REGINA (*slowly, nods*). When did you find out the bonds were gone?

HORACE. Wednesday night.

REGINA. I thought that's what you said. Why have you waited three days to do anything? (*Suddenly laughs.*) This will make a fine story.

HORACE (*nods*). Couldn't it?

REGINA (*still laughing*). A fine story to hold over their heads. How could they be such fools? (*Turns to him.*)

HORACE. But I'm not going to hold it over their heads.[7]

REGINA (*the laugh stops*). What?

HORACE (*turns his chair to face her*). I'm going to let them keep the bonds—as a loan from you. An eighty-eight thousand-dollar loan; they should be grateful to you. They will be, I think.

REGINA (*slowly, smiles*). I see. You are punishing me. But I won't let you punish me. If you won't do anything, I will. Now. (*She starts for door.*)

HORACE. You won't do anything. Because you can't. (*Regina stops.*) It won't do you any good to make trouble because I shall simply say that I lent them the bonds.

REGINA (*slowly*). You would do that?[8]

HORACE. Yes. For once in your life I am tying your hands. There is nothing for you to do. (*There is silence. Then she sits down.*)[9]

REGINA. I see. You are going to lend them the bonds and let them keep all the profit they make on them, and there is nothing I can do about it. Is that right?

HORACE. Yes.

REGINA (*softly*). Why did you say that I was making this gift?

HORACE. I was coming to that. I am going to make a new will, Regina, leaving you eighty-eight thousand dollars in Union Pacific bonds. The rest will go to Zan.[10] It's true that your brothers have borrowed your share for a little while. After my death I advise you to talk to Ben and Oscar. They won't admit anything and Ben, I think, will be smart enough to see that he's safe. Because I knew about the theft and said nothing.

6. What tone of voice would reveal Horace's feelings toward Regina's family?

7. In what tone would Horace say this?

8. How would Regina's voice change here?

9. What would be each character's manner during the silence? How would Regina move to sit?

10. Their daughter.

Nor will I say anything as long as I live. Is that clear to you?

REGINA (*nods, softly, without looking at him*). You will not say anything as long as you live.

HORACE. That's right. And by that time they will probably have replaced your bonds, and then they'll belong to you and nobody but us will ever know what happened. (*Stops, smiles.*) They'll be around any minute to see what I am going to do. I took good care to see that word reached Leo. They'll be mighty relieved to know I'm going to do nothing and Ben will think it all a capital joke on you. And that will be the end of that. There's nothing you can do to them, nothing you can do to me.

REGINA. You hate me very much.

HORACE. No.

REGINA. Oh, I think you do. (*Puts her head back, sighs.*) Well, we haven't been very good together. Anyway, I don't hate you either. I have only contempt for you. I've always had.

HORACE. From the very first?

REGINA. I think so.

HORACE. I was in love with *you*. But why did *you* marry *me*?

REGINA. I was lonely when I was young.

HORACE. *You* were lonely?

REGINA. Not the way people usually mean. Lonely for all the things I wasn't going to get. Everybody in this house was so busy and there was so little place for what I wanted. I wanted the world. Then, and then —(*Smiles.*) Papa died and left the money to Ben and Oscar.

HORACE. And you married me?

REGINA. Yes, I thought—But I was wrong. You were a small-town clerk then. You haven't changed.

HORACE (*nods, smiles*). And that wasn't what you wanted.

REGINA. No. No, it wasn't what I wanted. (*Pauses, leans back, pleasantly.*) It took me a little while to find out I had made a mistake. As for you—I don't know. It was almost as if I couldn't stand the kind of man you were—(*Smiles, softly.*) I used to lie there at night,

Courtesy of the William-Alan Landes Collection. **The Little Foxes** (l to r) Horace (Carroll O'Connor) and Regina (Lee Grant).

praying you wouldn't come near —

HORACE. Really? It was as bad as that?

REGINA (*nods*). Remember when I went to Doctor Sloan and I told you he said there was something the matter with me and that you shouldn't touch me any more?

HORACE. I remember.

REGINA. But you believed it. I couldn't understand that. I couldn't understand that anybody could be such a soft fool. That was when I began to despise you.

HORACE (*puts his hand to his throat, looks at the bottle of medicine on table*). Why didn't you leave me?

REGINA. I told you I married you for something. It turned out it was only for this. (*Carefully.*) This wasn't what I wanted, but it was something. I never thought about it much but if I had (**HORACE** *puts his hand to his throat.*) I'd have known that you would die before I would. But I couldn't have known that you would get heart trouble so early and so bad. I'm lucky, Horace. I've always been lucky. (**HORACE** *turns slowly to the medicine.*) I'll be lucky again. (**HORACE** *looks at her. Then he puts his hand to his throat. Because he cannot reach the bottle he moves the chair closer. He reaches for the medicine, takes out the cork, picks up the spoon. The bottle slips and smashes on the table. He draws in his breath, gasps.*)[11]

HORACE. Please. Tell Addie[12] — The other bottle is upstairs. (**REGINA** *has not moved. She does not move now. He stares at her. Then, suddenly as if he understood, he raises his voice. It is a panic-stricken whisper, too small to be heard outside the room.*) Addie! Addie! Come — (*Stops as he hears the softness of his voice. He makes a sudden, furious spring from the chair as if he were a desperate runner. On the fourth step he slips, gasps, grasps the rail, makes a great effort to reach the landing. When he reaches the landing, he is on his knees. His knees give way, he falls on the landing, out of view.* **REGINA** *has not turned during his climb up the stairs. Now she waits a second. Then she goes below the landing, speaks up.*)

REGINA. Horace. Horace. (*When there is no answer, she turns, calls.*) Addie! Cal! Come in here. (*She starts up the steps.*)[13]

11. The symptoms leading to Horace's attack must build in intensity. How does Regina react to them?

12. Addie is a servant whom Horace trusts.

13. In what tone would Regina call her husband's name? In what manner would she start toward him?

from
THE LITTLE FOXES
ACT 3
Lillian Hellman

It is the spring of 1900, the large living room of the Giddens house in a small Southern town. A wide circular staircase leads to the second floor. (See page 35 for further background.)

Horace Giddens, a wealthy banker, has died of a heart attack while his wife, Regina, stood by refusing to help. After Giddens' death Regina attempts to blackmail her brothers with their theft of some bonds from Giddens' safe-deposit box. She hopes to force her brothers to give her seventy-five percent of the profit from the investment of the bonds.

At the opening of the following scene, Regina's brother, Ben, has just gone out, slyly implying that Giddens' death has not yet been fully explained. Regina is alone with her daughter, Alexandra. Alexandra has always been a meek, easily dominated girl.

> **REGINA** (*sits quietly for a second, stretches, turns to look at* **ALEXANDRA**). What do you want to talk to me about Alexandra?
>
> **ALEXANDRA** (*slowly*). I've changed my mind. I don t want to talk. There's nothing to talk about now.
>
> **REGINA.** You're acting very strange. Not like yourself. You've had a bad shock today. I know that. And you loved Papa, but you must have expected this to come some day. You knew how sick he was.
>
> **ALEXANDRA.** I knew. We all knew.
>
> **REGINA.** It will be good for you to get away from here. Good for me, too. Time heals most wounds, Alexandra. You're young, you shall have all the things I

Courtesy of the American Conservatory Theatre. **The Little Foxes** Alexandra (Heidi Helen Davies).

wanted. I'll make the world for you the way I wanted it to be for me. (*Uncomfortable.*)[1] Don't sit there staring. You've been around Birdie[2] so much you're getting just like her.

ALEXANDRA (*nods*). Funny. That's what Aunt Birdie said today.

REGINA (*nods*). Be good for you to get away from all this. . . . We'll go in a few weeks. A few weeks! That means two or three Saturdays, two or three Sundays. (*Sighs.*) Well, I'm very tired. I shall go to bed.[3] You go to your room, Alexandra. Addie[4] will bring you something hot. You look very tired. (*Rises.*) I don't want to see anybody else. I don't want any condolence calls tonight. The whole town will be over.

ALEXANDRA. Mama, I'm not coming with you. I'm not going to Chicago.[5]

REGINA (*turns to her*). You're very upset, Alexandra.

ALEXANDRA (*quietly*). I mean what I say. With all my heart.

REGINA. We'll talk about it tomorrow. The morning will make a difference.[6]

ALEXANDRA. It won't make any difference. And there isn't anything to talk about. I am going away from you. Because I want to. Because I know Papa would want me to.

REGINA (*puzzled, careful, polite*). You *know* your papa wanted you to go away from me?

ALEXANDRA. Yes.

REGINA (*softly*). And if I say no?

ALEXANDRA (*looks at her*). Say it, Mama, say it. And see what happens.

REGINA (*softly, after a pause*).[7] And if I make you stay?

ALEXANDRA. That would be foolish. It wouldn't work in the end.

REGINA. You're very serious about it, aren't you? (*Crosses to stairs.*) Well, you'll change your mind in a few days.

ALEXANDRA. You only change your mind when you want to. And I won't want to.[8]

REGINA (*going up the steps*). Alexandra, I've come to the end of my rope. Somewhere there has to be what I

1. In what ways might Regina show her discomfort?

2. Wife of Regina's brother, Oscar. Of an aristocractic Southern family, Birdie's openness and cultured interests contrast with the greedy machinations of her husband and his family.

3. How might Alexandra react when Regina announces that she is retiring?

4. A servant.

5. How would Alexandra say this?

6. Should Regina's voice reveal her true feelings here?

7. What might be happening during the pause? How would Regina look at Alexandra?

8. Which words would be emphasized here?

9. Alexandra's speech leads to a climax. Where is the high point of the speech? How does she build to it?

10. How would Regina be reacting to Alexandra's change in nature?

11. In the last two speeches and the business involved with them, what is revealed about the characters and the relationship between them? How does the scene reveal this pictorially? What vocal inflections does Alexandra use in her last line?

want, too. Life goes too fast. Do what you want; think what you want; go where you want. I'd like to keep you with me, but I won't make you stay. Too many people used to make me do too many things. No, I won't make you stay.

ALEXANDRA [9]You couldn't, Mama, because I want to leave here. As I've never wanted anything in my life before. Because now I understand what Papa was trying to tell me. (*Pause.*) All in one day: Addie said there were people who ate the earth and other people who stood around and watched them do it. And just now Uncle Ben said the same thing. Really, he said the same thing. (*Tensely.*) Well, tell him for me, Mama, I'm not going to stand around and watch you do it. Tell him I'll be fighting as hard as he'll be fighting (*Rises.*) some place where people don't just stand around and watch.[10]

REGINA. Well, you have spirit, after all. I used to think you were all sugar water. We don't have to be bad friends. I don't want us to be bad friends, Alexandra. (*Starts, stops, turns to* **ALEXANDRA**.) Would you like to come and talk to me, Alexandra? Would you — would you like to sleep in my room tonight?

ALEXANDRA (*takes a step towards her*). Are you afraid, Mama? (**REGINA** *does not answer. She moves slowly out of sight.*)[11]

from
LADIES IN RETIREMENT
ACT 1, SCENE 2
Edward Percy and Reginald Denham

I t is a June morning, 1885. The action is set in the living room of Estuary
House, a large pre-Tudor farmhouse near a small English town in the
Thames marshes. There is a huge open hearth. In the chimney wall is the
iron door of a baking oven. A large lattice window allows light to pour into
the room, which contains an assortment of Victorian furniture, antiques, and
bric-a-brac.

Miss Leonora Fiske is in her sixties, but her manner is active and youthful.
It is obvious that she wears cosmetics and an auburn wig. She is quick of wit
and temper. Her companion and housekeeper is Ellen Creed. Ellen is
younger than Leonora, dignified, and dresses plainly. She is almost hand-
some.

Ellen's senile sisters have been staying at Leonora's house. They have convinced themselves that the house actually belongs to Ellen and that Leonora
must leave. The sisters, Louisa and Emily, appear at the end of this scene
after a confrontation between Leonora and Ellen.

From "Ladies in Retirement" by Edward Percy and Reginald Denham. Published by English Theatre Guild
Limited.

LEONORA (*crosses Right Center*). I'm sorry I was so put out, Ellen. But there's a limit to patience, you know.

ELLEN. It's I who should have apologized.

LEONORA. Nonsense, dear. I mustn't expect you to be responsible for your sisters.[1]

ELLEN. But I am responsible for them.

LEONORA. I don't want to add to your troubles, and I know what a burden they are; but . . .

ELLEN. Oh, but, Leonora, they're no burden at all. When my father was dying he made them over to me. They're a sacred trust—just as if they were my children. I've always looked after them. I've supported them. Every penny I earn goes to them.

LEONORA (*crosses to piano—starts to polish*).[2] My dear, you must be either a saint or a fool!

ELLEN. But what would become of them if I didn't? You see, when I had the shop and it failed, I lost their little money as well as my own. Everything they have is invested in me, and I must give them some dividend.

LEONORA. But you're forgetting that I haven't been brought up with them. They haven't been made over to me. And, while you may be used to them, I find them impossible to have about the house. (*Dusts keys.*)

ELLEN. They have been a little naughty today, I admit. (*Crosses to stairs.*) But I'll give them a good talking to, and then everything will be all right.[3]

LEONORA (*firmly*). That won't do, Ellen. I'm trying to tell you, as kindly as I can, that they've got to go.

ELLEN (*she seems stunned*). To go? When? (*There is a pause.*)[4] When do you want them to go?

LEONORA. At once. This week. I can't stand them any longer. I'm at the end of my tether.

ELLEN (*crosses to front of table Center*). I don't know how I shall break it to them.

LEONORA (*growing exasperated*). But I only invited them here for a few weeks. Didn't they understand that? They've been here nearly four months.

ELLEN. Oh, no! Surely not as long as that?

LEONORA. They came at the beginning of June, and now we're well into September. And another thing.

1. Both are polite. Are they honest? What is the tone and manner of each?

2. How is the action affected when Leonora begins to polish the piano?

3. What is Ellen's tone? What is she trying to suggest about her sisters' behavior?

4. What is Leonora's facial expression during the pause?

(*Crosses to* ELLEN.) I don't think you've been quite fair to me. You never told me they were — well, what they are.

ELLEN. I told you they were rather pathetic.

LEONORA. Yes, my dear; but pathetic's not next door to insane.

ELLEN (*almost savagely*). They're not insane![5]

LEONORA. Naturally, you put the best side of the picture forward. They're your own flesh and blood. But, insane or pathetic or whatever you choose to call them, they've overstayed their welcome. I won't have them here any longer. (*Crosses with polish and duster, puts them on landing.*)

ELLEN. It's your house, I know. But you'll have to give me a little time.

LEONORA. What's time got to do with it?

ELLEN. Well, I don't quite know where I'll be able to send them.

LEONORA (*crosses down from landing*). But surely they've only got to get into a train and go back where they came from?

ELLEN. No. I didn't keep on their room.

LEONORA (*crosses to* ELLEN). But, my dear! You knew they weren't coming here on a visit for life!

ELLEN. I didn't want the expense. Besides, I hoped that perhaps you might have taken to them more than you have. I hoped we might be able to arrange something. It's a large house. There are several empty rooms. I was going to suggest that I should pay you something out of my wages toward their keep.

LEONORA. Oh, you were, were you? And is that why Louisa made that odd remark just now?

ELLEN. What odd remark?

LEONORA. That you'd promised her she should stay through the winter!

ELLEN. I never promised her.

LEONORA. I suspected something of the sort at the time.

ELLEN. I said I never promised her.[6]

LEONORA. Very well, I accept that.

ELLEN. I admit I didn't realize quite how you felt.

You've never given an inkling of it.

LEONORA. My dear Ellen, are you quite blind? You must have seen that I've got more and more exasperated.

ELLEN. I thought we might have gone on as we were for a little longer.

LEONORA. Well, you know how I feel now. I hope you realize we can't. This little holiday has come to an end. (*Crosses to piano.*)

ELLEN (*sits Right of table*). You make me feel my position very much. I suppose you want me to go, too?[7]

LEONORA. My dear Ellen, of course not! We got on like a house on fire before they came. I don't regard you, dear, as my servant. I think of you as my friend. You know my pillar-to-post career hasn't made me any permanent ones. Mine's a lonely existence. Terribly lonely. It's bound to be. And I've no family—no relations to fall back on. (*Crosses to above table.*) So, you see, I value your companionship. More, perhaps, than you realize. I definitely don't want you to go.

ELLEN (*rises, crosses to sofa down Right*). I'm afraid it won't be altogether easy to forget what you think about my sisters. Or that you turned them out when they were so happy.[8]

LEONORA (*crosses to* **ELLEN**). But I haven't turned them out! Their visit's just come to its end in the normal way. That's all.

ELLEN. Things can never be quite the same, can they?

LEONORA. Ellen! Don't tell me that you're crazy, too! For goodness' sake, try to see this thing sensibly. Don't you realize that you're being frightfully unreasonable?

ELLEN (*sits on sofa*). People who've got all they want never understand how much the smallest thing means to those who haven't.

LEONORA (*getting very angry*). Really! I don't think this calls for a sermon on charity! I've been more than generous to you and your sisters.

ELLEN. But it's a little cruel to give with one hand only to take away with the other.

LEONORA. Oh, my goodness! You're beginning to

7. How do the women's situations in life differ? Why might Ellen refer to this? What is the effect of Ellen sitting at this moment? What is her tone of voice?

8. What is Ellen trying to do? How is it consistent with her previous actions? What is the tone and rate of her speech?

make me wish I'd never given at all! (*Crosses Center.*)

ELLEN. People have always been very generous to you, Leonora. You've got a home. You've got investments. You've got your one or two — allowances, haven't you?

LEONORA. Well, what of it? (*Crosses up Left, paces about room.*)

ELLEN. My sisters and I — we haven't any gentlemen to send us money.

LEONORA. That's hardly my fault, is it?

ELLEN. No, but don't you ever feel that you have a special responsibility to women like us?

LEONORA (*still moving about*). I don't know what you're talking about![9]

ELLEN. Don't you owe a debt to virtue? I've had to work for the money I've made. But at least I've kept my self-respect.

LEONORA (*raging. Crosses Right to* **ELLEN**). How dare you? How dare you criticize my life? Do you think it hasn't been slavery to get the little I've got? Do you think it's cost me nothing but a few cheap embraces? How can you, a dried-up old spinster — how can you understand anything of what my life's been? Do you think I haven't had my torments? Do you think I don't envy women who've got respectability, who've got families, who aren't just forgotten or pensioned off when they lose their stock-in-trade?[10]

ELLEN. Then you can't blame me for fighting for my family!

LEONORA. Ellen, you're a hypocrite. You're worse. You're a cheat. You've pretended to be my friend. But it wasn't friendship you felt for me. You meant to batten on me and get the utmost out of me. You wanted to foist your wretched brood on me indefinitely. You wanted to manoeuvre me into a false position and bleed me white. And when I saw through your little scheme you had the insolence to turn on me and abuse me. But you've chosen the wrong woman! (*Going to the kitchen door.*) I suggest you take a month's wages and go. (*She stands looking at the seated* **ELLEN**. *She is shaking with rage. Then to her amazement*

9. What should Leonora's activity reveal about her feelings?

10. How might Leonora's building anger be shown? Where is the climax of her speech?

ELLEN *crumples up. She bursts into tears.*)

ELLEN. Leonora, don't go like that. Don't go, please. I'm absolutely in the wrong. I didn't mean half I said. I'm dreadfully sorry.

LEONORA (*still quivering*). I should hope you are!

ELLEN. You're quite right about my sisters. They are — peculiar. I don't wonder they've got on your nerves. I think perhaps they've got on mine, too, and that's why I said what I did. But, you see, I love them. I love them intensely — just because they are so helpless. They're almost a religion with me. You're quite right, though, Leonora. They can't stay here. They must go. I see that. I'll send them away. I'll arrange it at once. Only don't send me away, too. I've been so happy here. And I promise everything shall be the same as before. Only don't send me away.

(**LEONORA** *moved but still hurt.*)

LEONORA. Well, I think we'd better both sleep on it, Ellen. (*Then she goes quietly and quickly out into the kitchen.*)[11]

(*Almost immediately the door at the foot of the stairs opens and* **LOUISA** *and* **EMILY** *steal in. Like wicked children, they have obviously been listening. They come softly to either side of the sofa where* **ELLEN** *is still sitting. They look rather like three witches as they whisper together.*)

LOUISA. Ellen, we've been listening. Isn't she terrible, Ellen? She's wicked. Are you going to send us away? You promised you wouldn't, you know.

ELLEN (*putting her arms round them*). No, I'm not going to send you away.

EMILY. She spoils everything. I wish she could go!

LOUISA. But, Ellen, if you're not going to send us away, what are you going to do, Ellen?

ELLEN (*her face is distraught*). I don't know. I shall have to think.

LOUISA. Dear Ellen! Always so clever.

11. The scene may be cut here. However, what effect does the appearance of the sisters have on the scene?

from
LADIES IN RETIREMENT
ACT 3, SCENE 1
Edward Percy and Reginald Denham

I t is early in the fall of 1885, the living room of Estuary House in Sussex. The baking oven in the chimney wall has recently been bricked over. (See page 43 for further background.)

Ellen Creed had been Leonora Fiske's housekeeper and companion in Estuary House. Ellen had invited her homeless, senile sisters, Louisa and Emily, to visit her in Estuary House. But when the visit had lengthened and shown no signs of ending, Leonora had demanded that Ellen remove her sisters. Having had nowhere to send the childlike women, and feeling herself obliged to protect them, Ellen had then murdered Leonora and sealed her body in the baking oven.

Ellen and her sisters have remained in Estuary House as though nothing had happened. Albert Feather, Ellen's nephew, is now also staying in Estuary House. He is a dapper, unctuous young thief who is hiding from the police. Ellen has told him that Leonora is away visiting. Albert, however, has begun to sense that Ellen is not telling the truth. Remarks made by Lucy, the maid with whom Albert pretends to be in love, have increased his suspicion of Ellen. Ellen, sympathetic to Albert earlier, now feels threatened and wants to be rid of him as soon as possible. In this scene Lucy has just run out as Ellen enters and finds Albert.

From "Ladies in Retirement" by Edward Percy and Reginald Denham. Published by English Theatre Guild Limited.
CAUTION: All rights are strictly reserved. Inquiries for amateur rights, in the United States and Canada, should be addressed to Dramatists Play Service, Inc., 440 Park Avenue South, New York, New York 10016. Inquiries for professional rights and inquiries for amateur rights outside the United States and Canada should be addressed to English Theatre Guild Limited, Ascot House, 52 Dean Street, London, W. 1, England.

1. What tone of voice, gestures, movements will make Albert appear jaunty?

2. What vocal quality and physical manner will reveal Ellen's feelings toward Albert?

3. Ellen and Albert have begun to spar, each slyly and subtly attacking the other's position and defending his own. What is Ellen's motive? Albert's motive? What is the tempo of their exchanges? What kinds of words would receive particular emphasis?

(**ELLEN** *comes downstairs. There is a look on her face which shows she is ready to give battle.*)

ALBERT (*crosses Right. Jauntily*).[1] Well, Auntie, where's your cane? From the way you spoke I thought you were going to take down my breeches and give me a dozen.

ELLEN. Don't you wish you could pay for your misdeeds that way?[2]

ALBERT (*sits right of table*). You take me too seriously, you know. Half the time I'm only fooling.

ELLEN (*crosses to Left of table*). One has to take a thief seriously.

ALBERT (*with a shrug*). Oh, come, Auntie! We don't want to go all over that again, do we? I'm not proud of myself. (*With a swift glance.* **ELLEN** *sits at table.*) We're all miserable sinners, aren't we? You used to tell me that often enough when I was a little boy. I'm not going about in sackcloth and ashes for the rest of my life!

ELLEN (*beginning to toy with her supper*). I've been to London today.

ALBERT (*with interest*). Have you? Why didn't you tell us? What, have you been on the spree?

ELLEN. No. I've been on your account. I've been to a shipping company.

ALBERT (*wide-eyed*). A shipping company—on my account?

ELLEN. Yes. I've bought your passage to Canada.

ALBERT (*up in arms*). But I don't want to go to Canada.

ELLEN (*coldly*). I don't think you've very much choice, have you?

ALBERT (*half jauntily this time*). I'm quite happy here for the time being.[3]

ELLEN (*very directly*). I'm not quite happy having you here.

ALBERT. But I thought we'd agreed. I was to lie low till the Gravesend business blew over. Time enough for a passage abroad in a month or so.

ELLEN. I've changed my mind.

ALBERT. Well, I think you might have discussed it with me first.

ELLEN. I didn't see any need. I'm paying the piper.

ALBERT. But what's made you change your mind?

ELLEN. Well, in the first place, you play the fool so much with Louisa and Emily that you'll have them chattering about your being here. And you know what that'll mean. The wrong sort of word to the tradesmen or the nuns and we shall have the police down on us. And I can't do with any scandal here.

ALBERT (*protestingly*). Oh, but isn't that a bit thin? They're not very difficult to keep an eye on.

ELLEN. You forget Emily goes for long walks. You don't know who she talks to.

ALBERT. But surely there's more to it than that, Auntie? There must be!

ELLEN. Yes. There's Lucy. She's even more dangerous than your aunts.

ALBERT. Oh, Lucy won't give me away.

ELLEN (*catching at this*). Are you in a position to be sure?

ALBERT (*very surprised*). What do you mean?

ELLEN. You know well enough what I mean. You wouldn't mind adding Lucy to your conquests, would you?

ALBERT (*with exaggerated innocence*). It never so much as occurred to me. I've hardly noticed the girl.

ELLEN. Don't lie, Albert. I've watched you whispering together. I saw the way you eyed her the first evening you came. I've seen her setting her cap at you ever since. I'm not going to have that sort of thing going on under my roof!

ALBERT. Well, all I can say, Auntie, is—it must be your mind. We're as innocent as the driven snow.

ELLEN (*with suppressed rage*). You hateful little hypocrite!

ALBERT. Can't one have a joke and a bit of a lark with a girl without being accused of ruining her?

ELLEN (*sharply*). I never said you'd ruined her. Have you? Am I a little behindhand in sending you away?

ALBERT (*protestingly once more*). Now look here. If you go on talking to me like this, I shall get quite cross. I'm doing my best to keep my temper as it is.[4]

ELLEN (*contemptuous*). Your temper! You can't pull

4. What is Albert trying to do here? How would his voice and gestures show it?

wool over my eyes, Albert! Now, listen. You'll start tomorrow. I'm coming with you. Bates will be here directly after breakfast.

ALBERT (*now thoroughly alarmed*). But I daren't go up to London! I might be recognized.

ELLEN. You're not going to London. Bates will drive up to Maidstone. Then we'll make our way across country by coach to Southampton. There's a boat leaving for Quebec on Friday. I've got your ticket. I've got everything.

ALBERT (*grumblingly*). By Jove, you are a hard woman, Auntie.

ELLEN. Perhaps I am. Perhaps circumstances have made me so. And you haven't helped to make me any softer.

ALBERT. I don't know why you're suddenly so down on me.

ELLEN (*quietly, but with great bitterness*). I've got to know you better. I've watched you very carefully the last few days. You're not a bit sorry for what you've done. You haven't shown a spark of gratitude to me. You're thoroughly callous. You've demoralized your aunts. Goodness knows what harm you've done to that young girl. You've nosed about the house and spied on everybody. If I hadn't put my cash box in a very secure place I'm quite sure your light fingers would have found a way to it. And I'm saying this to my sister's son!

ALBERT (*half whimpering*). You are full of the milk of human kindness, aren't you? I suppose you realize I've never had a chance — brought up as I was. It's not my fault if I'm ambitious.

ELLEN (*scornfully*). Ambitious!

ALBERT. Yes. Ambitious. I don't want to be downed all my life — with other people's footmarks all over me. I want to be on top. (*Rises.*) And I'm going to be!

ELLEN. Well, you're not going to climb there on my shoulders. I've made up my mind, and it's no use arguing with me. (*Rises.*) You're going out of this house before you're a day older.

ALBERT (*plucking up his courage*). I see. That's what you think. Does it occur to you that I may not go?

ELLEN. Well, I can't throw you out physically, but I can always send for the police. (*Crosses Left.*)

ALBERT. Somehow I'd got the impression you didn't want the police here.

ELLEN (*turning to* **ALBERT**). Does that mean you refuse to go?

ALBERT. Well, I certainly shan't go tomorrow morning.

ELLEN. I'm afraid you'll have to.

ALBERT (*crosses to fireplace*). No. On second thoughts I'm quite content to stay for the time being. I'm getting fond of the place. The air suits me. (*Sits Right of hearth.*) You can't bluff me, you know.

ELLEN (*angrily. Crossing up Right to him*). I'm not bluffing you, Albert. I'm ordering you to go.

ALBERT. Order—my foot! I'll tell you what I think of your reasons for wanting me out of the house. Bunkum.

ELLEN. What do you mean?

ALBERT. There's another you haven't mentioned, isn't there? A sounder one.

ELLEN (*pacing up to the issue*). Yes. There is.

ALBERT. Ah, now we're getting down to brass tacks! It's about Miss Fiske, isn't it?

ELLEN. Yes, it is. (*Quite naturally.*)⁵ I met her in town today. She's coming back.

ALBERT (*absolutely staggered*). You met her in town, you say?

ELLEN. Yes. Why shouldn't I?

ALBERT (*nonplussed*). No reason.

ELLEN (*watching him closely*). I had to take her some money that came for her.

ALBERT. I'd got it into my head that she'd gone for good.

ELLEN. Who gave you that idea? It's her house. There's never been any question of her not coming back.

ALBERT. Well, in that case, why spend the last half hour abusing me? Why not tell me straightaway I'd got to go because she was coming back?

ELLEN (*crosses, sits Left of hearth*). I didn't want you to

5. A transition in mood. Does Ellen relax? What gestures and/or movements will show her feelings?

know anything about it.

ALBERT. Why not?

ELLEN. You're such a chatterbox. You'd go blurting it out to your aunts. And it would be fatal if they got to know about it now. Because—don't you see?—it means that they've got to go, too. And I shall have to break it to them very gently.

ALBERT (*rises. Almost convinced*). Oh, well—there's nothing for it, then. My little country holiday has obviously come to an end. I'll have to thank you for your loving care, Auntie, and kiss you good-bye. I don't know what the blazes I'll do in Canada. But I suppose one can starve there as well as anywhere else.[6]

6. What is Albert's manner now?

ELLEN. I shall give you something to start on. I can't do less—for Rose's sake. (*Rises.*) I've no doubt you'll pick up a living somehow. There's a bit of the Greek in you, Albert. He thrives where the Jew starves, you know.

ALBERT. I'll do my best to deserve your good opinion, Auntie. And I suppose I ought to be grateful.

ELLEN (*crosses to desk*). I'm not asking for that.

ALBERT. Well, I'd better get some sleep, hadn't I? I'm going to have a tiring day tomorrow. (*He has risen. A sudden thought strikes him, and, while closely watching her, he knocks out his pipe on the bake-oven door. The tap-tap of the wood on the metal sounds extraordinarily sinister. It is as if somebody inside were knocking. ELLEN turns with a little shudder. ALBERT comes forward.*)[7] Do we kiss good night?

7. Timing is important here. What is the facial expression of each character during this business?

ELLEN. No.

ALBERT (*looking into her drawn face*). I say! You're looking rather played out. Hadn't you better toddle off, too?

ELLEN (*with an effort*). I'm just coming. I've got to lock up. (*She crosses to Right.*)

(ALBERT *goes to the stairway. Then he turns.*)

ALBERT. Oh, Auntie, I had a funny dream last night.

ELLEN (*turning to him*). What was that?

ALBERT. I dreamt Miss Fiske was dead.

ELLEN (*facing him coolly*). Oh?

ALBERT. Good night. (*He goes upstairs.*)[8]

8. What mood or feeling should Albert's last line and departure create?

from
STAGE DOOR
ACT 1, SCENE 2
Edna Ferber and George S. Kaufman

I t is late at night in November. The action takes place in a bedroom in the Footlights Club, a club in the theater district of New York for girls trying to break into professional acting. Through a narrow window one glimpses the city lights and part of a large electric sign.

The play is about the lives of sixteen girls seeking careers in the theater. It focuses mainly on Terry Randall. Terry has a bright personality and an expressive face but has just lost her job in a play which closed suddenly. She shares her room in the Footlights Club with Kaye Hamilton, a rather ethereal girl with an air of vulnerability, and Jean Maitland, who does not appear in this excerpt. In this scene Terry and Kaye have just been left alone by some friends who had tried to cheer them up.

This scene and the scene immediately following it in this book are part of a single scene from the original play and may, therefore, be played contiguously. They have been separated here to allow the actors to focus on each of the situations individually and to afford the possibility of more actors becoming involved in a variety of scenes.

(**KAYE** *and* **TERRY** *are alone. With a sigh* **TERRY** *again faces reality. Listlessly she begins to undress.* **KAYE** *is almost ready for bed. As she turns back bedclothes she pauses to regard* **TERRY**.)

1. Terry's
boyfriend.

2. How would
Terry's voice,
gestures,
movements project
this mood?

3. A friend who
returned home to
marry a stable
person.

KAYE. I know how sunk you feel, Terry. It's that horrible letdown after the shock has worn off.

TERRY. The idiotic part of it is that I didn't feel so terrible after the first minute. I thought, well, Keith's[1] coming around after the show, and we'll go to Smitty's and sit there and talk and it won't seem so bad. But he never showed up.

KAYE. Terry, I shouldn't try to advise you where men are concerned. I haven't been very smart myself —but this isn't the first time he's let you down. Don't get in too deep with a boy like Keith Burgess. It'll only make you unhappy.

TERRY. I don't expect him to be like other people. I wouldn't want him to be. One of the things that makes him so much fun is that he's different. If he forgets an appointment it's because he's working and doesn't notice. Only I wish he had come tonight. (*She is pulling her dress over her head as she talks and her words are partly muffled until she emerges.*) I needed him so. (*Suddenly her defenses are down.*)[2] Kaye, I'm frightened. For the first time, I'm frightened. It's three years now. The first year it didn't matter so much. I was so young. Nobody was ever as young as I was. I thought, they just don't know. But I'll get a good start and show them. I didn't mind anything in those days. Not having any money, or quite enough food; and a pair of silk stockings always a major investment. I didn't mind because I felt so sure that that wonderful part was going to come along. But it hasn't. And suppose it doesn't next year? Suppose it never comes?

KAYE. You can always go home. You've got a home to go to, anyhow.

TERRY (*rises*). And marry some home-town boy—like Louise?[3]

KAYE. I didn't mean that, exactly.

TERRY. I can't just go home and plump myself down on Dad. You know what a country doctor makes? When I was little I never knew how poor we were, because mother made everything seem so glamorous—so much fun. (*Starts Left for bathroom—all this* *time* **TERRY** *has continued her preparations for bed; hung up her dress, slipped her nightgown over her head.*) Even if I was sick it was a lot of fun, because then I was allowed to look at her scrapbook. I even used to pretend to be sick, just to look at it—and that took acting, with a doctor for a father. (*Exits and makes rest of change off stage continuing dialogue.*) I adored that scrap-book. All those rep-company[4] actors in wooden attitudes—I remember a wonderful picture of mother as Esmeralda. It was the last part she ever played, and she never finished the performance.[5]

KAYE. What happened?[6]

TERRY. She fainted, right in the middle of the last act. They rang down and somebody said, "Is there a doctor in the house?" And there was. And he married her.

KAYE. Terry, how romantic!

TERRY. Only first she was sick for weeks and weeks. Of course the company had to leave her behind. They thought she'd catch up with them any week, but she never did.

KAYE. Didn't she ever miss it? I mean afterward.

TERRY (*coming back into room, crosses Right to bureau*). I know now that she missed it every minute of her life. I think if Dad hadn't been such a gentle darling, and not so dependent on her, she might have gone off and taken me with her. I'd have been one of those children brought up in dressing rooms, sleeping in trunk trays, getting my vocabulary from stage-hands. (*As she creams her face.*)

KAYE. That would have been thrilling.

TERRY. But she didn't. She lived out the rest of her life right in that little town, but she was stage-struck to the end. There never was any doubt in her mind—I was going to be an actress. It was almost a spiritual thing, like being dedicated to the church.

KAYE. I never thought of the theatre that way. I just used it as a convenience, because I was desperate, and now I'm using it again because I'm desperate.

TERRY. Oh, now I've made you blue. I didn't mean to be gloomy. We're fine! We're elegant! They have to

4. Repertoire acting company.

5. Terry's recollection changes the mood of the scene. What vocal quality and manner would be appropriate?

6. How might Kaye dramatize her interest?

pay me two weeks' salary for this flop. Eighty dollars.
We're fixed for two weeks. One of us'll get a job.

KAYE. I can't take any more money from you. You paid
my twelve-fifty last week.

TERRY. Oh, don't be stuffy! I happened to be the one
who was working.

KAYE. I'll never get a job. I'm — I'm not a very good actress.

TERRY. Oh, now!

KAYE. And there's nothing else I can do and nobody I
can go back to. Except somebody I'll *never* go back to.

TERRY. It's your husband, isn't it?

KAYE (*looks at* TERRY *a moment, silently*). I ran away from
him twice before, but I had to go back. I was hungry,
and finally I didn't even have a room. Both times, he
just waited. He's waiting now.[7]

TERRY. Kaye, tell me — what is it? Why are you afraid
of him?

KAYE (*turns her eyes away from* TERRY *as she speaks*). Because I know him. To most people he's a normal attractive man. But I know better. Nights of terror.
"Now, darling, it wouldn't do any good to kill me.
They wouldn't let you play polo tomorrow. Now,
we'll open the window and you'll throw the revolver
at that lamp-post. It'll be such fun to hear the glass
smash." And then there were the times when he
made love to me. I can't even tell you about that. (*She
recalls the scene with a shudder.*)[8]

TERRY. Kaye, darling! But if he's as horrible as that,
can't you do something legally?

KAYE (*a desperate shake of her head*). They have millions.
I'm nobody. I've gone to his family. They're united
like a stone wall. They treated me as though I was
the mad one.

TERRY. But, Kaye, isn't there anybody — What about
your own folks? Haven't you got any?

KAYE. I have a father. Chicago. I ran away at sixteen
and went on the stage. Then I met Dick — and I fell
for him. He was good-looking, and gay, and always
doing sort of crazy things — smashing automobiles
and shooting at bar-room mirrors. . . . I thought it

7. The focus
changes to Kaye.
What changes does
this call for in the
manner of each
character?

8. Kaye recalls
vividly. Where is her
emphasis? How
would her voice
reveal her feelings
about her past?

was funny, *then*.

TERRY. And I've been moaning about my little troubles.

KAYE. You know, I'd swore to myself I never was going to bother you with this. Now, what made me do it!

TERRY. I'm glad you did. It'll do you good.

KAYE. Yes, I suppose it will.

TERRY (*as she takes counterpane off bed*). Well, we might as well get those sheep over the fence. Maybe we'll wake up tomorrow morning and there'll be nineteen managers downstairs, all saying, "You and only you can play this part."

KAYE. I suppose Jean'll be out till all hours.[9]

TERRY (*at window, puts up shade—electric sign comes on one-quarter up*). There's a girl who hasn't got any troubles. Life rolls right along for her. . . . (*Puts up window.*) Well, ready to go bye-bye?

KAYE (*switches off all lights except bed lamps—electric sign up to one-half*). I suppose I might as well. But I feel so wide awake.

(*As* **TERRY** *opens a window a blast of noise comes up from the street. A cacophony made up of protesting brakes, automobile horns, taxi drivers' shouts, a laugh or two. From her dresser* **KAYE** *takes a black eyeshield and adjusts it over her eyes after she is in bed.* **TERRY** *does same, then shouts a Good night! loudly enough to be heard above the street din.* **KAYE'S** *Good night is equally loud. Simultaneously they turn out their bed lights. For a second—but only a second —the room is in darkness. Then the reason for* **TERRY'S** *eyeshade becomes apparent. A huge electric advertising sign on an adjacent roof flashes on, off, on, off, full up, alternately flooding the room with light and plunging it into darkness.*)

TERRY (*shouting*). Funny if we both *did* get jobs tomorrow!

KAYE. Huh?

TERRY (*louder*). I say, it would be funny if we both got jobs tomorrow!

KAYE. Certainly would.

9. Jean Maitland. What should this line reveal about Kaye's feelings toward Jean?

from
STAGE DOOR
ACT 1, SCENE 2
Edna Ferber and George S. Kaufman

I t is late at night, a bedroom in the Footlights Club in New York. (See page 55 for further background.)

Terry Randall, Kaye Hamilton, and Jean Maitland are neophyte actresses who share a room in the Footlights Club. Terry has just lost her job in a play which closed suddenly. Kaye sympathizes with Terry, knowing that Terry is the most devoted actress among the three roommates. In this excerpt Terry and Kaye have retired for the night after trying to boost each other's spirit. They have been in bed only a few moments when Jean Maitland enters. Jean is beautiful and vivacious. She is an opportunist with immense appeal to men.

(A moment of silence. The door bursts open. JEAN comes in, bringing with her a quiver of excitement. She is in dinner clothes.)

JEAN *(turns on light full up except bed lamps and bureau lamp. Electric sign dims one-half)*. Terry! Wake up!

1. How would the voices of the two girls differ?

TERRY. What's the matter?[1]

JEAN *(slams window down—street noise stops)*. We're in the movies!

TERRY. What?

The introductory paragraphs on this page have been added by the present editors and are not a part of the original play.

JEAN. Both of us! We're in the movies! They just heard from the Coast.

TERRY. Jean! How do you know? What happened?

JEAN. Mr. Kingsley[2] just got the telegram. They liked the tests, and we're to go to the office tomorrow to sign our contracts. We leave for the Coast next week! Terry! Can you believe it!

KAYE. Oh, girls, how exciting![3]

TERRY (*bewildered*). Yes. Yes. You mean—right away?

JEAN. Of course we'll only get little parts in the beginning. But there's that beautiful check every week, whether you work or not. And the swimming and the sunshine and those little ermine jackets up to here. No more running around to offices and having them spit in your eye. And a salary raise every six months if they like us. So at the end of three years it begins to get pretty good, and after five years it's wonderful, and at the end of seven years it's more money than you ever heard of.[4]

TERRY. Seven years! What do you mean—seven years!

JEAN. Yes, it's a seven-year contract—that is, if they take up the options.

TERRY. But what about the stage? Suppose I wanted to act?

JEAN. Well, what do you think this is—juggling? Motion picture acting is just as much of an art as stage acting, only it's cut up more. You only have to learn about a line at a time, and they just keep on taking it until you get it right.

TERRY (*staring at* **JEAN***. A stricken pause. Then she shakes her head slowly. Her decision is made*). Oh, no.

JEAN. What?

TERRY. I couldn't.

JEAN. Couldn't what?

TERRY. That isn't acting, that's piecework. You're not a human being, you're a thing in a vacuum. Noise shut out, human response shut out. But in the theatre, when you hear that lovely sound out there, then you know you're right. It's as though they'd turned on an electric current that hit you here. And that's how you learn to act.[5]

2. A movie producer.

3. Kaye and Terry had been nearly asleep. How would their coming to awareness be shown convincingly?

4. How would the quality of Jean's voice vary as she imagines the future and contrasts it with the present?

5. How would Terry's tone and gestures differ from Jean's in describing a movie actress's life?

JEAN. You can learn to act in pictures. You have to do it till it's right.

TERRY. Yes, and then they put it in a tin can, like Campbell's Soup. And if you die the next day it doesn't matter a bit. You don't even have to be alive to be in pictures.

JEAN. I suppose you call *this* being alive! Sleeping three in a room in this rotten dump. It builds you up, eh?

TERRY. I'm not going to stay here all my life. This is only the beginning.

JEAN. Don't kid yourself. You've been here three years, and then it's three years more, and then another three and where are you? You can't play ingenues forever. Pretty soon you're a character woman, and then you're running a boarding house like old Orcutt. *That'll* be nice, won't it?[6]

TERRY. I don't know. You make me sound like a fool, but I know I'm not. All I know is I want to stay on the *stage*. I just don't want to *be* in pictures. An actress in the theatre, that's what I've wanted to be my whole life. It isn't just a career, it's a feeling. The theatre is something that's gone on for hundreds and hundreds of years. It's—I don't know—it's part of civilization.[7]

JEAN. All right, you stay here with your civilization, eating those stews and tapiocas they shove at us, toeing the mark in this female seminary, buying your clothes at Klein's. That's what you like, eh?

TERRY. *Yes*, I like it!

JEAN. And I suppose you like this insane racket going on all night!

(*She throws open window—street noises start.*)

TERRY (*yelling above noise*). Yes, I *do*![8]

JEAN. And that Cadillac car sign going on and off like a damned lighthouse! (*She turns off light. Again we see the flash of electric sign, off, on, off, on, full up and flashing faster.*) I suppose you've got to have that to be an actress!

TERRY. Yes! Yes! Yes! Yes! Yes!

JEAN (*not stopping for her*). Well, not for me. I'm going out where there's sunshine and money and fun

6. What might Kaye be doing while the girls argue?

7. What gestures or movement would be appropriate here?

8. The following exchanges between Jean and Terry overlap and run together. At what points would they break in on each other?

and —

TERRY (*shouting above her*). And little ermine swimming pools up to here!

(*The street noise, the flashing light, and their angry shouts are still going on as curtain descends.*)[9]

JEAN (*as curtain falls*). I'm going to make something out of my life. I'm not going to stay in this lousy dump.

9. What action might be appropriate to each character as the curtain falls?

from
A RAISIN IN THE SUN
ACT 1, SCENE 1
Lorraine Hansberry

It is a Friday morning in spring, the 1950's. The living room-kitchen of the Younger family is on Chicago's South Side. Three generations of the family live in the apartment. The apartment is neat but shabby and crowded. Worn upholstery has been partially masked with crocheted doilies. Furniture has been moved to hide bald spots in the carpet. There is a single window.

After the death of Walter Younger, his family has found that it has conflicting plans for the insurance money he left. Mama Younger wants to buy a house in a better community. Walter, her son, wants to open a liquor store. Walter's sister, Beneatha, would like to use some of the money for college. Ruth, Walter's wife, shares Mama's desire to buy a house. Though only thirty, Ruth has few expectations and no illusions. Mama, who is in her sixties, is a strong and noble woman. In the scene which follows, Mama and Ruth have been doing household chores and discussing their plans for the insurance money when Beneatha enters.

(BENEATHA *comes in, brushing her hair and looking up to the ceiling, where the sound of a vacuum cleaner has started up.*)

BENEATHA. What could be so dirty on that woman's rugs that she has to vacuum them every single day?

RUTH. I wish certain young women 'round here who I

From A RAISIN IN THE SUN, by Lorraine Hansberry. Copyrights © 1958 by Robert Nemiroff as Executor of the estate of Lorraine Hansberry as an unpublished work. Copyright © 1959, 1966 by Robert Nemiroff as Executor of the estate of Lorraine Hansberry. Reprinted by permission of Random House, Inc. and William Morris Agency, Inc.

could name would take inspiration about certain rugs in a certain apartment I could also mention.

BENEATHA (*shrugging*). How much cleaning can a house need, for Christ's sakes.

MAMA (*not liking the Lord's name used thus*). Bennie!

RUTH. Just listen to her—just listen!

BENEATHA. Oh, God!

MAMA. If you use the Lord's name just one more time—

BENEATHA (*a bit of a whine*). Oh, Mama—

RUTH. Fresh—just fresh as salt, this girl!

BENEATHA (*drily*). Well—if the salt loses its savor—[1]

MAMA. Now that will do. I just ain't going to have you 'round here reciting the scriptures in vain—you hear me?

BENEATHA. How did I manage to get on everybody's wrong side by just walking into a room?

RUTH. If you weren't so fresh—

BENEATHA. Ruth, I'm twenty years old.

MAMA. What time you be home from school today?

BENEATHA. Kind of late. (*With enthusiasm.*) Madeline is going to start my guitar lessons today.

(**MAMA** *and* **RUTH** *look up with the same expression.*)

MAMA. Your *what* kind of lessons?

BENEATHA. Guitar.

RUTH. Oh, Father!

MAMA. How come you done taken it in your mind to learn to play the guitar?

BENEATHA. I just want to, that's all.

MAMA (*smiling*). Lord, child, don't you know what to do with yourself? How long it going to be before you get tired of this now—like you got tired of that little play-acting group you joined last year? (*Looking at* **RUTH**.) And what was it the year before that?

RUTH. The horseback-riding club for which she bought that fifty-five-dollar riding habit that's been hanging in the closet ever since!

MAMA (*to* **BENEATHA**). Why you got to flit so from one thing to another baby?

BENEATHA (*sharply*). I just want to learn to play the guitar. Is there anything wrong with that?

MAMA. Ain't nobody trying to stop you. I just wonders

1. How do the manners of Ruth and Beneatha differ? What should this reveal about each character?

sometimes why you has to flit so from one thing to another all the time. You ain't never done nothing with all that camera equipment you brought home—

BENEATHA. I don't flit! I—I experiment with different forms of expression—

RUTH. Like riding a horse?

BENEATHA. —People have to express themselves one way or another.

MAMA. What is it you want to express?

BENEATHA (angrily). Me! (MAMA and RUTH look at each other and burst into raucous laughter.) Don't worry—I don't expect you to understand.[2]

MAMA {to change the subject). Who you going out with tomorrow night?

BENEATHA (with displeasure). George Murchison again.

MAMA (pleased). Oh—you getting a little sweet on him?

RUTH. You ask me, this child ain't sweet on nobody but herself—(Underbreath.) Express herself! (They laugh.)

BENEATHA. Oh—I like George all right, Mama. I mean I like him enough to go out with him and stuff but—

RUTH (for devilment). What does and stuff mean?

BENEATHA. Mind your own business.

MAMA. Stop picking at her now, Ruth. (A thoughtful pause, and then a suspicious sudden look at her daughter as she turns in her chair for emphasis.) What does it mean?

BENEATHA (wearily). Oh, I just mean I couldn't ever really be serious about George. He's—he's so shallow.

RUTH. Shallow—what do you mean he's shallow? He's rich![3]

MAMA. Hush, Ruth.

BENEATHA. I know he's rich. He knows he's rich, too.

RUTH. Well—what other qualities a man got to have to satisfy you, little girl?

BENEATHA. You wouldn't even begin to understand. Anybody who married Walter could not possibly understand.

MAMA (outraged). What kind of way is that to talk about your brother?

BENEATHA. Brother is a flip—let's face it.

MAMA (to RUTH, helplessly). What's a flip?

RUTH (glad to add kindling). She's saying he's crazy.

BENEATHA. Not crazy. Brother isn't really crazy yet — he — he's an elaborate neurotic.

MAMA. Hush your mouth!

BENEATHA. As for George. Well. George looks good — he's got a beautiful car and he takes me to nice places and, as my sister-in-law says, he is probably the richest boy I will ever get to know and I even like him sometimes — but if the Youngers are sitting around waiting to see if their little Bennie is going to tie up the family with the Murchisons, they are wasting their time.

RUTH. You mean you wouldn't marry George Murchison if he asked you someday? That pretty, rich thing? Honey, I knew you was odd —

BENEATHA. No I would not marry him if all I felt for him was what I feel now. Besides, George's family wouldn't really like it.

MAMA. Why not?

BENEATHA. Oh, Mama — the Murchisons are honest-to-God-real-*live*-rich colored people, and the only people in the world who are more snobbish than rich white people are rich colored people. I thought everybody knew that. I've met Mrs. Murchison. She's a scene!

MAMA. You must not dislike people 'cause they well off, honey.

BENEATHA. Why not? It makes just as much sense as disliking people 'cause they are poor, and lots of people do that.

RUTH (*a wisdom-of-the-ages manner. To* **MAMA**). Well, she'll get over some of this —

BENEATHA. Get over it? What are you talking about, Ruth? Listen, I'm going to be a doctor. I'm not worried about who I'm going to marry yet — if I ever get married.

MAMA *and* **RUTH.** *If!*

MAMA. Now, Bennie —

BENEATHA. Oh I probably will[4] . . . but first I'm going to be a doctor, and George, for one, still thinks that's pretty funny. I couldn't be bothered with that. I am going to be a doctor and everybody around here bet-

4. How is this transition in thought shown vocally and physically?

ter understand that!

MAMA (*kindly*). 'Course you going to be a doctor, honey, God willing.

BENEATHA (*drily*). God hasn't got a thing to do with it.

5. A climax begins here. Where is the peak of this action?

MAMA. Beneatha—that just wasn't necessary.[5]

BENEATHA. Well—neither is God. I get sick of hearing about God.

MAMA. Beneatha!

BENEATHA. I mean it! I'm just tired of hearing about God all the time. What has He got to do with anything? Does He pay tuition?

6. What business and movement might be appropriate here?

MAMA. You 'bout to get your fresh little jaw slapped.![6]

RUTH. That's just what she needs, all right!

BENEATHA. Why? Why can't I say what I want to around here, like everybody else?

MAMA. It don't sound nice for a young girl to say things like that—you wasn't brought up that way. Me and your father went to trouble to get you and Brother to church every Sunday.

BENEATHA. Mama, you don't understand. It's all a matter of ideas, and God is just one idea I don't accept. It's not important. I am not going out and be immoral or commit crimes because I don't believe in God. I don't even think about it. It's just that I get tired of Him getting credit for all the things the human race achieves through its own stubborn effort. There simply is no blasted God—there is only man and it is he who makes miracles! (MAMA *absorbs this speech, studies her daughter and rises slowly and crosses to* BENEATHA *and slaps her powerfully across the face. After, there is only silence and the daughter drops her eyes from her mother's face, and* MAMA *is very tall before her.*)

MAMA. Now—you say after me, in my mother's house there is still God. (*There is a long pause and* BENEATHA *stares at the floor wordlessly.* MAMA *repeats the phrase with precision and cool emotion.*) In my mother's house there is still God.

7. What facial expressions might be appropriate during the pause?

BENEATHA. In my mother's house there is still God. (*A long pause.*)[7]

MAMA (*walking away from* BENEATHA, *too disturbed for triumphant posture. Stopping and turning back to her daughter*). There are some ideas we ain't going to have in this house. Not long as I am at the head of this family.

BENEATHA. Yes, ma'am.

(MAMA *walks out of the room.*)

RUTH (*almost gently, with profound understanding*). You think you a woman, Bennie—but you still a little girl. What you did was childish—so you got treated like a child.

BENEATHA. I see. (*Quietly.*) I also see that everybody thinks it's all right for Mama to be a tyrant. But all the tyranny in the world will never put a God in the heavens! (*She picks up her books and goes out.*)

RUTH (*goes to* MAMA'S *door*). She said she was sorry.

MAMA (*coming out, going to her plant*). They frightens me, Ruth. My children.

RUTH. You got good children, Lena. They just a little off sometimes—but they're good.

MAMA. No—there's something come down between me and them that don't let us understand each other and I don't know what it is. One done almost lost his mind thinking 'bout money all the time and the other done commence to talk about things I can't seem to understand in no form or fashion. What is it that's changing, Ruth?

RUTH (*soothingly, older than her years*). Now . . . you taking it all too seriously. You just got strong-willed children and it takes a strong woman like you to keep 'em in hand.

MAMA (*looking at her plant and sprinkling a little water on it*). They spirited all right, my children. Got to admit they got spirit—Bennie and Walter. Like this little old plant that ain't never had enough sunshine or nothing—and look at it . . . (*She has her back to* RUTH, *who has had to stop ironing and lean against something and put the back of her hand to her forehead.*)

RUTH (*trying to keep* MAMA *from noticing*). You . . . sure . . . loves that little old thing, don't you? . . .

MAMA. Well, I always wanted me a garden like I used to see sometimes at the back of the houses down home. This plant is close as I ever got to having one.

(*She looks out of the window as she replaces the plant.*) Lord, ain't nothing as dreary as the view from this window on a dreary day, is there? Why ain't you singing this morning, Ruth? Sing that "No Ways Tired." That song always lifts me up so—(*She turns at last to see that* **RUTH** *has slipped quietly into a chair, in a state of semiconsciousness.*) Ruth! Ruth honey—what's the matter with you . . . Ruth!

Courtesy of Author's Collection. **A Raisin in the Sun** (l
to r) Ruth (Ruby Dee), Mama (Claudia McNeil), Travis
(Glynn Turman), Walter (Sidney Poitier), and Karl (John
Fiedler).

Courtesy of Author's Collection. **A Raisin in the Sun** (l
to r) Walter (Sidney Poitier), Mama (Claudia McNeil),
Ruth (Ruby Dee), Travis (Glynn Turman), and Beneatha
(Diana Sands).

from
A RAISIN IN THE SUN
ACT 3
Lorraine Hansberry

It is late summer, the 1950's. On Chicago's South Side the Younger apartment is stacked with packing crates. A few items of necessary furniture remain. (See page 64 for further background.)

The insurance money which Mama Younger received after her husband's death has caused problems. The partner of Mama's son, Walter, has absconded with the $6500 Mama had given Walter. $3000 of that sum had been intended for the college education of Walter's sister, Beneatha, who would like to become a doctor. Also, a representative of the Clybourne Improvement Association has indicated that the Youngers will not be welcomed into its community, where Mama has just purchased a house. Disappointed by these events, Beneatha is further confused about her personal life. She is being courted by two men, George Murchison, the son of a traditional and successful businessman, and Joseph Asagai, an idealistic Nigerian intellectual.

In this scene ". . . Beneatha sits at the table, still surrounded by the now almost ominous packing crates. She sits looking off. We feel that this is a mood struck perhaps an hour before, and it still lingers now, full of the empty sound of profound disappointment. . . ." The doorbell rings, and Beneatha goes to the door without feeling. Asagai enters, energetic, self-assured, smiling broadly.

> **ASAGAI.** I came over . . . I had some free time. I thought I might help with the packing. Ah, I like the look of packing crates! A household in preparation

1. What movements and gestures will help define Asagai's character?

2. What is the tone of Beneatha's voice?

3. Her brother's child.

4. How might the word "Me" be varied?

5. What are Beneatha's feelings about this past event? How would her voice reveal her feelings?

for a journey! It depresses some people . . . but for me . . . it is another feeling. Something full of the flow of life, do you understand? Movement, progress . . . It makes me think of Africa.[1]

BENEATHA. Africa![2]

ASAGAI. What kind of a mood is this? Have I told you how deeply you move me?

BENEATHA. He gave away the money, Asagai . . .

ASAGAI. Who gave away what money?

BENEATHA. The insurance money. My brother gave it away.

ASAGAI. Gave it away?

BENEATHA. He made an investment! With a man even Travis[3] wouldn't have trusted.

ASAGAI. And it's gone?

BENEATHA. Gone!

ASAGAI. I'm very sorry . . . And you, now?

BENEATHA. Me? . . . Me? . . . Me I'm nothing . . . Me.[4] When I was very small . . . we used to take our sleds out in the wintertime and the only hills we had were the ice-covered stone steps of some houses down the street. And we used to fill them in with snow and make them smooth and slide down them all day . . . and it was very dangerous you know . . . far too steep . . . and sure enough one day a kid named Rufus came down too fast and hit the sidewalk . . . and we saw his face just split open right there in front of us . . . And I remember standing there looking at his bloody open face thinking that was the end of Rufus. But the ambulance came and they took him to the hospital and they fixed the broken bones and they sewed it all up . . . and the next time I saw Rufus he just had a little line down the middle of his face . . . I never got over that . . .[5]

ASAGAI. What?

BENEATHA. That that was what one person could do for another, fix him up — sew up the problem, make him all right again. That was the most marvelous thing in the world . . . I wanted to do that. I always thought it was the one concrete thing in the world that a human being could do. Fix up the sick, you know—and make them whole again. This was truly being God . . .

ASAGAI. You wanted to be God?

BENEATHA. No—I wanted to cure. It used to be so important to me. I wanted to cure. It used to matter. I used to care. I mean about people and how their bodies hurt . . .

ASAGAI. And you've stopped caring?

BENEATHA. Yes—I think so.

ASAGAI. Why?

BENEATHA. Because it doesn't seem deep enough, close enough to what ails mankind—I mean this thing of sewing up bodies or administering drugs. Don't you understand? It was a child's reaction to the world. I thought that doctors had the secret to all the hurts. . . . That's the way a child sees things—or an idealist.[6]

ASAGAI. Children see things very well sometimes—and idealists even better.

BENEATHA. I know that's what you think. Because you are still where I left off—you still care. This is what you see for the world, for Africa. You with the dreams of the future will patch up all Africa—you are going to cure the Great Sore of colonialism with Independence—

ASAGAI. Yes![7]

BENEATHA. Yes—and you think that one word is the penicillin of the human spirit: "Independence!" But then what?[8]

ASAGAI. That will be the problem for another time. First we must get there.

BENEATHA. And where does it end?

ASAGAI. End? Who even spoke of an end? To life? To living?

BENEATHA. An end to misery![9]

ASAGAI (*smiling*). You sound like a French intellectual.

BENEATHA. No! I sound like a human being who just had her future taken right out of her hands! While I was sleeping in my bed in there, things were happening in this world that directly concerned me—and nobody asked me, consulted me—they just went out

6. Is Beneatha's disillusionment genuine? What quality of voice will best express her feelings?

7. What gestures and movements will emphasize Asagai's optimism?

8. Beneatha is seated. How might her voice, gestures, and posture be used to focus attention on her at appropriate moments?

9. Throughout the scene, timing of lines is important. When do the characters speak emotionally? When do they speak thoughtfully? How would this affect the tempo of their exchanges?

and did things—and changed my life. Don't you see there isn't any real progress, Asagai, there is only one large circle that we march in, around and around, each of us with our own little picture—in front of us—our own little mirage that we think is the future.

ASAGAI. That is the mistake.

BENEATHA. What?

ASAGAI. What you just said—about the circle. It isn't a circle—it is simply a long line—as in geometry, you know, one that reaches into infinity. And because we cannot see the end—we also cannot see how it changes. And it is very odd but those who see the changes are called "idealists"—and those who cannot, or refuse to think, they are the "realists." It is very strange, and amusing too, I think.

BENEATHA. You—you are almost religious.

ASAGAI. Yes . . . I think I have the religion of doing what is necessary in the world—and of worshipping man—because he is so marvelous, you see.

BENEATHA. Man is foul! And the human race deserves its misery!

ASAGAI. You see: *you* have become the religious one in the old sense. Already, and after such a small defeat, you are worshipping despair.

BENEATHA. From now on, I worship the truth—and the truth is that people are puny, small and selfish. . . .

ASAGAI. Truth? Why is it that you despairing ones always think that only you have the truth? I never thought to see *you* like that. You! Your brother made a stupid, childish mistake—and you are grateful to him. So that now you can give up the ailing human race on account of it. You talk about what good is struggle; what good is anything? Where are we all going? And why are we bothering?

BENEATHA. *And you cannot answer it!* All your talk and dreams about Africa and Independence. Independence and then what? What about all the crooks and petty thieves and just plain idiots who will come into power to steal and plunder the same as before—only now they will be black and do it in the name of new

Independence— You cannot answer that.

ASAGAI (*shouting over her*). *I live the answer!* (*Pause.*) In my village at home it is the exceptional man who can even read a newspaper . . . or who ever *sees* a book at all. I will go home and much of what I will have to say will seem strange to the people of my village . . . But I will teach and work and things will happen, slowly and swiftly. At times it will seem that nothing changes at all . . . and then again . . . the sudden dramatic events which make history leap into the future. And then quiet again. Retrogression even. Guns, murder, revolution. And I even will have moments when I wonder if the quiet was not better than all that death and hatred. But I will look about my village at the illiteracy and disease and ignorance and I will not wonder long. And perhaps . . . perhaps I will be a great man . . . I mean perhaps I will hold on to the substance of truth and find my way always with the right course . . . and perhaps for it I will be butchered in my bed some night by the servants of empire . . .[10]

BENEATHA. *The martyr!*[11]

ASAGAI. . . . or perhaps I shall live to be a very old man respected and esteemed in my new nation . . . And perhaps I shall hold office and this is what I'm trying to tell you, Alaiyo; perhaps the things I believe now for my country will be wrong and outmoded, and I will not understand and do terrible things to have things my way or merely to keep my power. Don't you see that there will be young men and women, not British soldiers then, but my own black countrymen . . . to step out of the shadows some evening and slit my then useless throat? Don't you see they have always been there . . . that they always will be. And that such a thing as my own death will be an advance? They who might kill me even . . . actually replenish me![12]

BENEATHA. Oh, Asagai, I know all that.

ASAGAI. Good! Then stop moaning and groaning and tell me what you plan to do.

BENEATHA. Do?

10. Asagai visualizes. How might this be dramatized?

11. What is Beneatha's tone of voice? What is her facial expression?

12. How does Beneatha's mood change during Asagai's speech? What is her facial expression as he speaks of Africa?

ASAGAI. I have a bit of a suggestion.

BENEATHA. What?

ASAGAI (*rather quietly for him*). That when it is all over—that you come home with me—

BENEATHA (*slapping herself on the forehead with exasperation born of misunderstanding*). Oh—Asagai—at this moment you decide to be romantic!

ASAGAI (*quickly understanding the misunderstanding*). My dear, young creature of the New World—I do not mean across the city—I mean across the ocean; home—to Africa.

BENEATHA (*slowly understanding and turning to him with murmured amazement*). To—to Nigeria?

ASAGAI. Yes! . . . (*Smiling and lifting his arms playfully.*) Three hundred years later the African Prince rose up out of the seas and swept the maiden back across the middle passage over which her ancestors had come—

BENEATHA (*unable to play*). Nigeria?

ASAGAI. Nigeria. Home. (*Coming to her with genuine romantic flippancy.*) I will show you our mountains and our stars; and give you cool drinks from gourds and teach you the old songs and the ways of our people—and, in time, we will pretend that—(*Very softly.*)—you have only been away for a day—(*She turns her back to him, thinking. He swings her around and takes her full in his arms in a long embrace which proceeds to passion.*)

BENEATHA (*pulling away*). You're getting me all mixed up—[13]

ASAGAI. Why?

BENEATHA. Too many things—too many things have happened today. I must sit down and think. I don't know what I feel about anything right this minute. (*She promptly sits down and props her chin on her fist.*)

ASAGAI (*charmed*). All right, I shall leave you. No—don't get up. (*Touching her, gently, sweetly.*) Just sit awhile and think . . . Never be afraid to sit awhile and think. (*He goes to door and looks at her.*) How often I have looked at you and said, "Ah—so this is what the New World hath finally wrought . . ." (*He exits.*)

BENEATHA *sits on alone.*)

13. What conflicting feelings is Beneatha experiencing?

from
THE OLD MAID
FIRST EPISODE
Zoe Akins

It is a few minutes before the hour set for Delia Lovell's wedding, a day in June, 1833. The scene is set in Delia's bedroom at her parents' country house overlooking the East River in New York.

Delia Lovell is the vain daughter of a wealthy family. She had been engaged to Clem Spender, an impoverished artist, but had broken the engagement to give Clem a year in which to become a financially successful artist and thereby worthy of her family ties. In his despair, and unknown to Delia, Clem turned briefly to Charlotte Lovell, Delia's cousin, for comfort. A child resulted from this affair, though no one but Charlotte knows of the child until later in the play. Despite her vanity, Delia continues to love Clem. Charlotte, too, is secretly in love with him.

As this scene begins Delia is soon to marry wealthy Jim Ralston. There is a knock on the door, and Charlotte calls from outside.

> CHARLOTTE. Delia!
> DELIA. Chatty?
> CHARLOTTE. May I come in?
> DELIA. Of course.
> CHARLOTTE (*crossing the room, to* DELIA, *importantly*). I've something for you.
> DELIA. How pretty you look! I never saw you look so well.
> (CHARLOTTE *laughs shortly, and then speaks simply.*)

From *The Old Maid* by Edith Wharton as dramatized by Zoe Akins. Copyright, 1934, 1935, by Edith Wharton and Zoe Akins. Published by Hawthorne Books, Inc.

1. What does this reaction reveal about Charlotte?

2. What is revealed here about Delia?

3. She picks up a garter from the table.

CHARLOTTE. Of course it's the dress.[1] (*She looks down at the dress gratefully.*) I don't often have a dress that's been especially made for me. Thank you for giving me this one.

DELIA (*carelessly*). Thank mamma. She wanted to see you dressed properly, of course.[2] . . . This is something borrowed.[3] (CHARLOTTE *politely turns away her head as* DELIA *puts on the garter. Then she continues, straightening up.*) You haven't anything blue I could carry, have you?

CHARLOTTE (*drawing a sharp breath*). It's odd you should ask me that. (*Looking at the small box in her hand.*) This is blue.

DELIA. What is it?

CHARLOTTE. A cameo. It's a present for you—from Clem Spender.

DELIA (*abruptly, startled*). From Clem! But—

CHARLOTTE. He asked me to give it to you. He unwrapped it to take out a note that was inside. That's how I saw it was a cameo, and blue. Then he changed his mind and gave me the note to give you, too.

DELIA. But I thought Clem was in Italy!

CHARLOTTE (*simply, but with a hard note in her voice*). He came home today. Just in time for your wedding. He hadn't heard you were going to marry someone else. He thought you must be ill because you'd stopped writing.

(*As* DELIA *opens the note,* CHARLOTTE *turns to go, but* DELIA *stops her before she can open the door.*)

DELIA. Wait—don't go!

(CHARLOTTE *turns from the door and stands waiting while* DELIA *reads the note. Then* CHARLOTTE *speaks again, very simply, but with the same hard note in her voice, as if she were steeling herself against saying more.*)

CHARLOTTE. They'll play the wedding march next.

DELIA. I know. (*Suddenly she covers her face with her hands and speaks impulsively.*) Oh Chatty, I'm afraid!

CHARLOTTE. Of what?

DELIA. Of Clem! Of what he may say or do. There'll be champagne, and if he should take a glass too much—.

Watch him, Chatty, will you? Be—be kind to him.

CHARLOTTE. I don't see how anyone could ever be unkind to poor Clem.[4]

DELIA (*bending her head, sharply*). Don't—!

CHARLOTTE (*coldly, but with some surprise*). I didn't know you cared that much.

DELIA. You knew I loved him.

CHARLOTTE. I knew you told him so.

DELIA. I must not cry.

CHARLOTTE. You won't cry if you keep saying to yourself, over and over: "I'm marrying a Ralston; I'm marrying a Ralston."[5]

DELIA (*defiantly, herself again*). Yes, I *am* marrying a Ralston; and I'm glad.

CHARLOTTE (*without sympathy*). Everyone's glad you're doing so well. They always expected you to, and you have. But I don't envy you, Delia.[6]

DELIA. I don't want you to envy me; but I don't want you to hold my marriage to Jim against me, either.

CHARLOTTE (*stubbornly*). When Clem went to Italy to study painting, two years ago, you promised to wait for him.

DELIA. I did wait—but if Clem wanted a wife, he should have stayed here and gone into his uncle's bank, and earned something.

CHARLOTTE. If he'd wanted you for his wife, he should have, of course. Trying to be an artist isn't the sort of thing you had any patience with.

DELIA. But I was patient. He promised to come back, if he failed, and go to work. And if he had, I'd have married him; even though papa disapproved. I swear that.

CHARLOTTE. It never occurred to you, I suppose, that an artist couldn't possibly know whether he was a failure or a success, at the end of a single year?

DELIA. I thought, and I still think, he should have known there was nothing in art, for him, by that time, and have come back and settled down. And he would have if he'd cared enough.

CHARLOTTE. He cared. You needn't think he didn't—

DELIA. You needn't think *I* didn't!

4. What is Charlotte's tone of voice?

5. What is Charlotte's tone here?

6. What movements and gestures might enliven the following exchanges?

CHARLOTTE (*with feeling*). Then why couldn't you have waited?

DELIA. I tell you I did wait! Not one year, but almost two. It was almost two years after Clem went away before I told Jim I'd marry him instead.

CHARLOTTE. Couldn't you have had the kindness, at least, to write Clem that you were going to marry someone else?

DELIA. I intended to. I—I—tried to.

CHARLOTTE. But you were ashamed.[7]

DELIA. No, I was not ashamed! I—(*Wavering a little.*) I'm fond of Jim. And it seemed hopeless to wait for Clem. (*Then frankly, unhappily.*) I couldn't bear to be an old maid, Chatty.

CHARLOTTE (*with a strange look of exaltation*). I shall be an old maid because the man I love doesn't love me. Not for any other reason.

DELIA (*frankly surprised; delicately; patronizingly*). Oh, Chatty—my dear! I'm so sorry. I didn't know there was anyone.

CHARLOTTE (*proudly, turning away from* DELIA'S *sudden glance*). No one has ever known. But I would have waited for him all my life.

DELIA. You think so, but life doesn't stop; one gets lonely; one wants children, and a home of one's own.

CHARLOTTE. I could have waited. (*Then she turns and goes to the door. There she pauses, listening. Then she turns back to* DELIA.) It's the wedding march![8]

DELIA (*with an effort*). I'm ready. (*Breathlessly.*) Remember, watch Clem.

CHARLOTTE. I'll not forget.

DELIA (*looking at the cameo*). "Something Blue." (*She slips it into the bosom of her dress, takes her bouquet, and moves across the room towards the door* CHARLOTTE *is holding open. There she pauses long enough to whisper, as she steadies herself by laying a hand on the other's arm.*) Oh Chatty—I'm trembling! (*But almost instantly she recovers her poise, and with her head lifted passes* CHARLOTTE, *disappearing into the passage outside, to the strains of the music, as the curtain falls.*)

7. On whom should be the focus of interest? What physical situation of the characters will help show this?

8. How might Charlotte react to hearing the wedding music?

from
THIEVES' CARNIVAL
ACT 2
Jean Anouilh
(translated by Lucienne Hill)

I t is an evening in the 1880's. The scene is set in the drawing room of a villa in France.

Gustave is one of a trio of thieves who masquerade as Spanish noblemen, hoping thereby to be admitted to the homes of the rich. When Lady Hurf invites the trio to her villa, young Gustave, who is ambitious but lacking in self-confidence, sees his chance to prove himself as a thief. Lady Hurf, however, is aware of the masquerade. She is titillated at the prospect of both entertaining and hoodwinking the thieves. For Lady Hurf the thieves are puppets with which she might relieve her perpetual boredom. But for Gustave and Juliette, Lady Hurf's niece, the fantasy results in a serious romantic involvement.

When the following scene opens, Gustave is alone with Juliette, pretending to be a nobleman named Don Pedro. Unable to reconcile his reluctant but increasing affection for Juliette with his ambition to rob her aunt's house, Gustave is not at ease. Though the part of Lord Edgar may be cut, it has been retained here for practice.

(*A drawing-room in* **LADY HURF'S** *house. It is evening, after dinner, and* **JULIETTE** *and* **GUSTAVE** *are sitting side by side; a little romantic air is heard in the distance.*)

JULIETTE. It's nice here. No one is disturbing us tonight.

GUSTAVE. Yes, it is nice.[1]

JULIETTE. For three days now you've been sad. Are you homesick for Spain?

GUSTAVE. Oh no.

1. How would Gustave's manner differ from Juliette's? How would his speech be affected by his feelings?

JULIETTE. I'm sorry now I wouldn't work at my Spanish at school. We might have spoken it together. It would have been fun.

GUSTAVE. I only speak a few words myself.

JULIETTE. Do you? That's funny.

GUSTAVE. Yes, it is rather.

(*A silence.*)

JULIETTE. It must be amusing to be a prince.

GUSTAVE. Oh, one gets used to it, you know.

(*A silence.*)

JULIETTE. Don Pedro, what's the matter? We were much friendlier three days ago.

GUSTAVE. Nothing's the matter.

(*A pause.* **LORD EDGAR** *crosses the room laden with papers.*)

LORD EDGAR (*muttering*). Though I should die in the endeavor, I'll set my mind at rest. (*He drops his papers. They jump up to help him but he bars path.*) Don't touch them! Don't touch them! (*He picks up the papers himself and goes out muttering.*) This momentous discovery, if discovery there be, must be surrounded with the greatest possible precautions.[2]

GUSTAVE. What is he looking for? He's done nothing but ferret about among those old papers since we came here.

JULIETTE. I don't know. He's a little mad. Only he's painstaking as well, you see, so sometimes the results are quite prodigious. (*A* **LITTLE GIRL** *comes in.*)[3] Oh, here's my little friend.

CHILD. Mademoiselle Juliette, I've picked some daisies for you.

JULIETTE. Thank you, darling.

CHILD. They haven't very many petals. Daddy says they aren't the ones that lovers use.

JULIETTE. Never mind.

CHILD. Shall I get some others?

JULIETTE. No. Yes. You're very sweet. (*She kisses her.*) Run away now. (*The* **CHILD** *goes.* **JULIETTE** *turns to* **GUSTAVE,** *shamefaced.*)

JULIETTE. Do you think it's silly of me?[4]

GUSTAVE. No.

JULIETTE. You said you loved me, Don Pedro, yet for

2. How do Gustave and Juliette react to Lord Edgar's business?

3. In practice, the little girl may be an off-stage voice. Juliette would have to mime the action.

4. What might Gustave be doing during Juliette's business with the little girl?

three days now you haven't even looked at me.

GUSTAVE. I do love you, Juliette.

JULIETTE. Then why—?

GUSTAVE. I can't tell you.

JULIETTE. My father wasn't titled, I know, but my aunt is a Lady, and my grandfather was an Honorable.

GUSTAVE. How funny you are. It isn't that.

JULIETTE. Do you think the Duke of Miraflores[5] would consent to my marrying you?

GUSTAVE (*smiling*). I'm sure he would.

JULIETTE. Why do you look so sad then, if you love me and everyone approves?

GUSTAVE. I can't tell you.

JULIETTE. But you do feel, don't you, that our lives might meet and join one day?

GUSTAVE. I would be lying if I told you I felt that.

JULIETTE (*turning away*). That's unkind of you.

GUSTAVE. Careful. Here's your cousin.

JULIETTE. Come into the garden. It's getting dark. I want you to tell me everything.[6] (*The music fades as they go.*)

5. Another thief, maquerading as Gustave's father.

6. In what manner would they exit? What is Gustave's facial expression?

from

THIEVES' CARNIVAL
ACT 3
Jean Anouilh
(translated by Lucienne Hill)

It is an evening in the 1880's, a drawing room of a villa in France. The room is dark. (See page 81 for further background.)

Gustave is a young thief who, by masquerading as a Spanish nobleman, has established himself as a guest in Lady Hurf's villa. He is ambitious but unsure of himself and wants to prove himself as a thief. He has also been reluctantly falling in love with Lady Hurf's niece, Juliette. When Lady Hurf puts on a thieves' carnival, a masquerade party for which the guests dress as thieves, Gustave summons his resolve and proceeds with his plan to rob the house. As this scene opens, Gustave appears in a darkened room in the villa and begins collecting loot.

1. How would their physical manners differ? How would the tones of their voices differ?

2. What gestures and movements would be appropriate during the following exchanges? At what points would they occur?

(**GUSTAVE** *appears and listens. He goes right round the room, examining its contents one by one. All of a sudden he flattens himself against the wall.*)

JULIETTE (*enters, dressed for a journey*). Here I am.

GUSTAVE. What are you doing here? Why didn't you go with the others?

JULIETTE. I've come to find you.

GUSTAVE. Get out of here, will you?[1]

JULIETTE. Why are you so harsh with me?

GUSTAVE. Go on, get out!

JULIETTE. I'll go, of course, if you don't want me, only I thought you would want me. What's the matter?

GUSTAVE. I've got a headache. I want to stay here.[2]

JULIETTE. Why this yarn, to me?

GUSTAVE. It isn't a yarn. Get out, will you? Go on, quick march!

JULIETTE. But—you've never spoken to me like this!

GUSTAVE. There's a first time for everything.

JULIETTE. What have I done?

GUSTAVE. Nothing in particular. It's too difficult to explain, and anyway you wouldn't understand.

JULIETTE. But, Señor Pedro . . .

GUSTAVE. There isn't any Señor Pedro, for a start. My name is Gustave. And secondly, will you please go away?

JULIETTE. And there was I thinking that you loved me—

GUSTAVE. We all make mistakes, don't we?

JULIETTE. But you used to tell me so.

GUSTAVE. I was lying.

JULIETTE. Oh, no! I don't believe it!

GUSTAVE (*going to her purposefully*) Listen, my little pet, I'm telling you to get out of here, double quick.[3]

JULIETTE. Why?

GUSTAVE. You'll see why later on. In the meantime go up to your room and weep over your lost illusions. (*He takes her arm to lead her to the door.*) What are you dressed up in this coat for? What kind of a costume is that meant to be?

JULIETTE. Traveling costume.

GUSTAVE. Traveling costume? You're mad.

JULIETTE. Please don't be angry. I came to find you so we could go away. You told me once we'd go away together.

GUSTAVE. I was joking. Anyway, how do you know I mean to go away?

JULIETTE. I know.

GUSTAVE. You look as though you know a lot of things. Come along with me.

JULIETTE. We might meet one of the servants in the passage. (*He looks at her.*) We'd better not move from here. We'll be quite safe in this room.

GUSTAVE. The Dupont-Duforts[4] must be waiting for you. Go and dress up as a pickpocket like the rest of them.

3. Gustave and Juliette are equally persistent. How is this shown in the voice and actions of each?

4. Guests at the carnival.

JULIETTE. Don't pickpockets ever wear traveling clothes?

GUSTAVE. You're not going to travel. You're going to a carnival.

JULIETTE. Once they've stolen, thieves go away as a rule. Why won't you let me come with you, since you're going away?

GUSTAVE (*seizes her*). You know too much, my girl!

JULIETTE. Oh, please, don't hurt me!

GUSTAVE. Don't be afraid. Just a precaution. (*He ties her to a chair, and searches in her handbag.*)

JULIETTE. Oh, don't rob my bag. There's nothing in it. Anyway, I give it to you.

GUSTAVE. Thank you. All I want is a handkerchief.

JULIETTE. What for?

GUSTAVE. To gag you with. (*He finds her handkerchief, which is microscopic.*) I ask you, what's the point of a handkerchief that size? Never mind, mine's clean.

JULIETTE. I'm not going to scream—I swear I won't scream—Señor Pedro! Gustave—Gusta . . . (*He gags her.*)

GUSTAVE. There. If you think this a Thieves' Carnival, my lass, you'll have to think again. I'm a real thief, I am. So is Hector, and so is the Duke of Miraflores. Except that those two, they're imbeciles as well. You've built yourself a castle in the air, that's all, and your aunt, who's got bats in her belfry, has built herself a dozen. But let me tell you *I* came to do a job, and I intend to do it.[5]

(*She struggles.*)

All right. All right. It's no good trying to soften me. I'm used to girls.

(*He begins to fill his sacks with the most unlikely objects in the room. After a while he looks at her with misgiving.*)

It's not too tight, is it?

(*She shakes her head.*)

That's a good girl. You see, old girl, I did a bit of billing and cooing, I know, but to be frank I didn't mean a word of it. I had to do it for the job.

(*She struggles again.*)

Does that upset you? Yes, I know, it isn't very pretty.

5. How convincing should Gustave's manner be? What is his facial expression?

But then in every trade there's always a little bit like that which isn't very pretty. Apart from that, I'm an honest sort of chap in my own way. I follow my trade, simply, without frills and fancies. Not like Hector and Peterbono. Peterbono has to be the Duke of Miraflores. One must be honest in one's own particular line. Life's not worth living otherwise.
(*He takes a furtive look at her.*)
You sure it's not too tight?
(*He gives her a smile.*)[6]
It worries me a bit, playing a trick like that on you, because you know, I lied just now. I am fond of you really.
(*He goes back to his work.*)
After all, when God invented thieves He had to deprive them of a thing or two, so He took away from them the esteem of honest folk. When you come to think of it, it's not so terrible. It could have been much worse.
(*He shrugs, and laughs, without daring to meet her eyes.*)
In a little while, you'll see, we'll have forgotten all about it.
(*He goes on collecting objects. She struggles again, and he looks at her.*)
If there's anything you care for specially, you must tell me. I'll leave it for you, as a souvenir. I mean, I'd *like* to give you a little present.
(*She looks at him and he stops in embarrassment.*)[7]
Please, don't look at me like that! You're breaking my heart! Can't you see I've got to do this? So just let me get quietly on with my job.
(*She moves.*)
Are you uncomfortable? You're not choking, are you? Look, Juliette, if you swear not to call out, I'll take the gag off. Do you swear?
(*She nods.*)
All right then, I trust you.
(*He removes the handkerchief.*)
What are you going to say to me, now that you know I'm a real thief? (*He sits down, resigned.*)
JULIETTE (*the moment she is ungagged*). This is absurd!

6. In this scene Gustave goes through a change of heart. How might this gradual occurrence be shown?

7. How would Juliette use her head and eyes to show her feelings?

Absolutely absurd. Untie me at once!

GUSTAVE. Oh, no! I'm a good sort, but business is business.

JULIETTE. At least listen to me!

GUSTAVE. What do you want to say?

JULIETTE. You don't imagine I came to find you, wearing my traveling coat, merely in order to sit here like a nincompoop bound and gagged in a chair? Of course I know you're a thief. If you weren't a real thief, I wouldn't have thought you were planning to leave in the middle of the night, would I, seeing you're a guest of my aunt's?[8]

GUSTAVE. What are you talking about?

JULIETTE. I've been telling you over and over again for the last hour. I love you. I saw you take a car out of the garage, I guessed you really were a thief, and that tonight was the night. As I supposed you'd go the moment the job was done, I dressed and got ready to go with you. You don't intend to stay, do you?

GUSTAVE. That's no question to ask a thief.

JULIETTE. Well then, take me with you.

GUSTAVE. But I'm a thief.

JULIETTE (*crying out in exasperation*). I tell you I know you're a thief! There's no need to go on and on about it. I wonder you don't draw attention to yourself. Come along untie my hands.

GUSTAVE. But, Juliette—

JULIETTE. Untie my hands. They're terribly painful.

GUSTAVE. Do you swear not to run away and raise the alarm?

JULIETTE. Yes, yes, I swear. Oh, how stupid you are!

GUSTAVE. I trust you of course, but I just don't understand. (*He unties her. She immediately powders her face, and then gets up with determination.*)

JULIETTE. We've wasted at least a quarter of an hour. Make haste. It wouldn't do to get caught now. Have you enough with this lot? (*She indicates the sacks with her foot.*)

GUSTAVE. What are you doing?

JULIETTE. Really, I shall begin to wonder if you're all

8. What is Gustave's facial expression during Juliette's rapid revelations?

there soon. Yes, or no, do I appeal to you?

GUSTAVE. Oh yes, but —

JULIETTE. Good. That's the main thing. Now, listen to me. Gustave, if you like me, I love you and I want to be your wife — oh, don't worry, if you're afraid of awkward questions at the Registry Office, we won't get properly married. There. Now then — (*She picks up one of the sacks.*) Is this all we're taking with us?

GUSTAVE (*snatching the sack from her*). Juliette, no! You don't know what you're doing! You mustn't come with me. What would become of you?

JULIETTE. I'd help you. I'd keep a look-out, and I'd whistle when I saw someone coming. I can whistle beautifully. Listen — (*She gives an earsplitting whistle.*)

GUSTAVE (*terrified*).[9] Ssssh! For heaven's sake! (*They listen for a moment.*)

JULIETTE (*humbly*). I'm sorry. What a fool I am. Take me away. I'll whistle very quietly, I promise you, and then only when it's absolutely necessary.

GUSTAVE. Juliette, this is only a whim. You're playing with me. It's unkind of you.

JULIETTE. Oh no, you mustn't think that! Never think that! I love you.

GUSTAVE. But do you know the dangers of this kind of life?

JULIETTE. Yes. Kiss me.

GUSTAVE. Juliette, it's good-bye to your tranquillity.

JULIETTE. It was on the way to killing me, my tranquillity. Kiss me.

GUSTAVE. But you're happy here, Juliette. You don't know what it means to be on the run, to be afraid. You're used to luxury.

JULIETTE. Why, we're rich! Look at this! If it worries you, we won't steal so long as the police are out looking for me.

GUSTAVE. Thieves aren't wealthy folk. You get precious little for what you sell.

JULIETTE. Well, we'll be poor then. Kiss me.

(*They join in a long kiss.*)

(*Radiantly.*) I am so happy. Now hurry. (*She stops.*) Why, you haven't taken the little Fragonards. You're

9. What action might be appropriate here?

mad, my darling, they're the most valuable things in the house. (*She runs to take them down.*) And the little enamels.[10](*She rummages in the sack.*) Leave the candlesticks. They're imitation bronze. You see how useful I am to you. I shall be such a help, you'll see. Kiss me.

GUSTAVE (*taking her in his arms again*). My little robber girl. (*They go.*)

10. What might Gustave be doing while Juliette is selecting?

from
EDWARD, MY SON
ACT 2, SCENE 3
Robert Morley and Noel Langley

I t is autumn, 1935. The scene is an expensively furnished hotel room in
Alassio on the Italian Riviera.

The play is about a father's thirty years of fanatical devotion to his son.
Though Edward, the son of Arnold and Evelyn Holt, does not appear in the
play, his off-stage presence initiates most of the action. Arnold Holt is a fasci-
nating tyrant, a great egotist whose resourcefulness, wit, and charm must be
admired despite his unscrupulous behavior. With his ruthless genius for
acquiring wealth and power, Arnold becomes an enormously successful businessman. Inspired only by his maniacal devotion to his son, Arnold sacrifices
his marriage and friends in advancing what he believes are Edward's best
interests. During her life with Arnold, Evelyn Holt changes from a happy,
romantic mother in the early scenes to a defensive and cynical middle aged
woman in the last.

When the following scene begins, Arnold has recently learned that his
wife has hired a detective to observe his activities. The purpose of the investigation is to obtain evidence of Arnold's affair with his secretary so that Evelyn can file for a divorce. As the scene opens, Evelyn is on the telephone.

EVELYN. Edward? . . . . Oh, I'm sorry. Yes, the luggage is ready but the car will have to wait. Mr. Edward
isn't back yet. Will you give me enquiries, please. . . .
Hullo, enquiries? It's Lady Holt speaking. Did you
ring the Aperitif? . . . and the Grand Hotel? Well,
he must be there. Will you try them again, please,
and the Tennis Club. . . . Yes, I know, but they

sometimes keep open later. He knew we were catching the seven-thirty . . . I'm so afraid there's been an accident. Yes . . . quite . . . thank you.

(She rings off. During the latter part of the conversation **ARNOLD** *has come into the room and stands quietly in the doorway. His clothes suggest that he has been travelling and are—as is everything about him now—slightly exaggerated.)*

ARNOLD. Good evening, my dear.

EVELYN. Arnold! What are you doing here?

ARNOLD. I have managed after all to snatch a few days' holiday. What could be more natural than that I should choose to spend them with my wife and child? Packing? I thought you'd booked your rooms here for another fortnight?

EVELYN. I changed my plans, Arnold.

ARNOLD. Really . . . and where were you thinking of hiding from me?[1]

EVELYN. Hiding from you! Don't be so absurd, I'd no intention of hiding.

ARNOLD. No. I rather thought that would be our Mr. Wilson's advice when he'd learnt I'd flown from Croydon. I must say there's something very satisfactory in being followed wherever one goes. It makes one feel quite young and romantic, like a character out of Sapper.[2]

EVELYN. I don't know what you're talking about.

ARNOLD. You don't read Sapper, perhaps. I wouldn't worry about Edward, if I were you, he's perfectly safe . . . at the pictures.

EVELYN. How do you know?[3]

ARNOLD. Because it was on my suggestion that he went there. I spoke to him on the telephone from Le Bourget this morning. I told him I planned to join you and wanted it to be a surprise. . . . I also suggested that the best way of delaying your departure was for him to disappear. I promised you wouldn't be angry at our little joke.

EVELYN. I am angry . . . but not with Edward. Like all your actions nowadays, I find it very underhand.

ARNOLD. I would call it underhand to have your hus-

---

1. The characters will be alternately attacking each other and defending themselves. Facial expressions, gestures, and movements are important since little physical drama takes place. Trace the progress of this confrontation. When is each character on the offensive? On the defensive? How would these changes of position be shown?

2. What is the tone of Arnold's voice? Wilson is a lawyer. Sapper was the pen name of Herman Cyril McNeile, a popular writer of crime and adventure stories.

3. What is Evelyn's reaction? How does it affect the manner of her speech?

band investigated by a private detective.

EVELYN. Perhaps I choose to fight you for once, Arnold, with your own weapons.

ARNOLD. But why bother to fight me at all? You won't win, you know.[4]

EVELYN. I wouldn't be too sure of that, Arnold. Mr. Wilson is very confident.

ARNOLD. Mr. Wilson is under the impression that the suit will be undefended, but he's wrong. I have no intention of giving you a divorce.

EVELYN. I'm delighted to hear you say so.

ARNOLD. Why?

EVELYN. Because I should like you to fight and lose — that is part of my plan for Edward.

ARNOLD. Your plan for Edward?[5]

EVELYN. I want him to realise that with all your money and power there are still some things you can't get away with.

ARNOLD. Why do you want a divorce?

EVELYN. Because I think it's the only way of bringing Edward to his senses.

ARNOLD. I don't know what you're talking about. What's the matter with Edward?[6]

EVELYN. A great deal, I'm afraid, at present, but nothing you'd understand.

ARNOLD. You might give me some indication.

EVELYN. Very well, I'll try. Take last night, for instance. Edward got very drunk last night. Then he was very sick. He was very rude to everyone, including a waiter. This morning I told him to apologise. He did. He gave the waiter five pounds. Now everyone in the hotel calls him "Milord." He's seventeen. If he goes on like this, what will he be like when he's twenty?

ARNOLD. Broke, I should think — the young devil. Why did you let him get tight?[7]

EVELYN. He slipped away to one of the bars in the Casino. He told me he was going to dance. He lies very fluently these days.

ARNOLD. Perhaps it wasn't a lie. Perhaps his girl stood

4. What is Arnold's manner?

5. Where is the emphasis in this line?

6. What is the tone of Arnold's voice? What is his reaction? What should it reveal about him?

7. How might Arnold's manner here reveal his reaction to Evelyn's story?

8. How would Arnold's attitude toward Edward be revealed by his voice and manner?

him up. Most kids get a little tipsy once, round about his age. It's not a bad thing; after that they lay off it.[8]

EVELYN. Edward doesn't lay off it. He goes on. He likes it. Like you, he doesn't see much harm in it.

ARNOLD. I don't see anything so very terrible in all this.

EVELYN. I know you don't, Arnold. That's the whole point. To you it's all rather a joke, isn't it? When I ask you to stop giving Edward money you promise and then you break your promise. I don't see things the way you do any more, I've suddenly woken up and I'm frightened, frightened for my son. That's why I'm going to take him away.

ARNOLD. Where are you thinking of taking him?

EVELYN. I don't know yet, but when I've divorced you, Arnold, I shall take Edward abroad somewhere. Somewhere where he can learn what it is to work for his living and to have responsibilities . . . I shall be one of those because I don't plan to take much money with me.

ARNOLD. You really think that Edward will agree to this fantastic scheme of yours?

EVELYN. Poor Edward. I'm afraid it will be an awful shock for him. But when I tell him that I don't want to touch your money and that I rely on him to look after me—well, I think he still loves me and he's not altogether lacking in courage or pride, you know.[9]

9. What quality in Evelyn's voice would reveal her feelings toward Edward?

ARNOLD. But even if you won this divorce you still couldn't take him out of England without my consent.

EVELYN. Mr. Wilson thinks that under the circumstances the Courts might give permission . . .

ARNOLD. Does he, indeed?

EVELYN. . . . and if you force me to stay in England I can always change my name. Mrs. Soames[10] did.

ARNOLD. Why do you hate me so much?

EVELYN. I don't hate you. I'm sorry. I shouldn't have said that about Mrs. Soames. I'm very tired. Do you mind if I go to bed?

ARNOLD. Go ahead. I'm still your husband. We're not divorced yet, you know.

10. Harry Soames, Arnold's first business partner, was imprisoned for illegal business practices and eventually committed suicide.

EVELYN. How long did you tell Edward to stay out?

ARNOLD. No particular time. I just wanted a chance to talk to you.

EVELYN. Now you've had that, perhaps you'll leave.

ARNOLD. Not just yet. Won't you sit down? Evelyn, I never realised that you cared so much. I thought that that side of marriage wasn't important to you nowadays. I'm not excusing what I've done—I'd have done it, I expect, whatever the circumstances might have been. I didn't realise that my taking a mistress would make you so terribly bitter. I'm sorry.

EVELYN. You haven't understood one word of what I've been saying, have you?

ARNOLD. Only that you think the best way of dealing with Edward is to break up his home.

EVELYN. His home! When did he last have a home? A real home? Something that wasn't a cross between the toy department of Harrod's and the Bank of England. Presided over by a perpetul fairy godfather who granted his every wish before he even thought of it himself.

ARNOLD. Some wives would be grateful to a husband who tried to be just that.

EVELYN. Possibly, but I'm not. I've had enough, Arnold. I've seen the fairy godfather when he's off duty. I think it's time Edward should too, time he got to know his father, and all his father stands for.

ARNOLD. You don't think it's rather late to introduce us? I think Edward knows a good deal more about me than you suspect. It's true he doesn't know about Eileen,[11] but I'm perfectly prepared that he should know if you really think it necessary. But while we're being so very frank with him, perhaps he should know about Larry[12] too.

EVELYN. What do you mean?[13]

ARNOLD. Larry's in love with you. I think you're in love with him. I think that's why you want a divorce.

EVELYN. You must be mad.

ARNOLD. Do you deny he's in love with you?

EVELYN. I really don't . . . of course it's quite absurd.

11. Arnold's secretary and mistress.

12. Larry Parker, a physician and friend of the Holts.

13. What is Evelyn's reaction to the change in the discussion? How does it affect her manner in the following exchanges?

ARNOLD. Is it? This will be a terrible thing for him, you know.

EVELYN. Why? What do you mean?

ARNOLD. You're his patient. The British Medical Council have very definite views about doctors who seduce their patients.

EVELYN. Are you accusing me of having an affair with Larry?

ARNOLD. No . . . and I sincerely hope you won't force me to do so.

EVELYN. You haven't a shred of evidence.

ARNOLD. No . . . not yet, perhaps. But you should know what private investigators can do once they start. This is going to be a very dirty case, you know. Are you quite sure you want to go on with it? Larry has been very good to us, very good to Edward. Whichever way the case goes, I'll see he gets plenty of publicity.

EVELYN. You're contemptible, Arnold. I don't think I've ever despised you as much as I do now.

ARNOLD. I'm not interested in what you feel any more. No matter what happens to us, I'll never forget that you wanted to take Edward away from me. There may be many things you can't forgive me for, this is one I'll never forgive you. I've always fought for Edward, I always will, and if you think I'm going to let you take him now and slander me and set him against me, you've made just about the biggest mistake of your life. This is my reward for what I've tried to do for you . . . tried to do for a wife who married me twenty years ago, who has waited her chance until she could strike and kill. Well, you haven't killed . . . your weapon was rather double-edged wasn't it? The question is, what are you going to do next?

EVELYN. I don't know. Please get out of here.

ARNOLD. Not until I have your promise that you'll stop this case.

EVELYN. Why should I? (*The telephone rings.*)

ARNOLD. Because I made the stakes a little too high.

You were never much of a gambler, were you? (*The telephone rings again. He picks up the receiver.*) Hello, yes. Oh yes. They want to know if you're staying on to-night. Are you? (*He puts a hand on her shoulder.*)[14]
EVELYN. Don't touch me!
ARNOLD. Yes, we're all staying. You may send my luggage up here. (*He puts down the receiver.*) Edward's back. I'd better go and look after him. He's just been a little sick in the lift.[15]

14. What is Evelyn's reaction to Arnold's question?

15. What emotions are expressed in Arnold's voice in this speech?

Courtesy of Robert Morley. **Edward, My Son** (l to r) Patricia Hicks and Robert Morley.

from

THE ENCHANTED
ACT 3
Jean Giraudoux
(adapted by Maurice Valency)

The play is set in the present, in a room in a provincial town in France. It has come to the attention of the authorities that there is something quite wrong in the small town in which *The Enchanted* is set. They are alarmed that the townspeople are too gay, too carefree, and do only what pleases them. The authorities send a supervisor to the town, charged with restoring normalcy to the town's life. The supervisor's investigation reveals that the cause of the town's poetic madness is a young schoolteacher, Isabel. In her desire to reform the world, Isabel has become acquainted with a ghost which tempts her with the adventure of death. Both the ghost and the supervisor become infatuated with Isabel. The ghost and the supervisor are opposing symbols in this allegorical fantasy. In the following scene the supervisor, knowing that the ghost is to appear, has come to Isabel's room.

1. Isabel is
unaccustomed to
seeing the
supervisor dressed
so formally.

(*The* SUPERVISOR *looks pale and very formal. He stands silent a moment, dressed in his Sunday best—black jacket, striped trousers, chamois gloves. He has a bowler hat in his right hand, a gold-headed stick in his left.* ISABEL *gazes at him in astonishment.*)[1]

SUPERVISOR. Not a word, if you please.

ISABEL. I don't know what to say.

SUPERVISOR. Don't say anything. Just listen.

ISABEL. Do you mind if I look?

SUPERVISOR. That is permitted. In fact, please do.

ISABEL. You look so grand.

SUPERVISOR. Don't poke fun at my finery. It is all that

sustains me at the moment. Except the thought of those who should be wearing it. They would certainly be here with me, if they were alive. As it is, let me present — my grandfather: his cane. My great-uncle: his watch and chain. My father: his hat. My Uncle Albert: his gloves. The rest is myself.

ISABEL. I am delighted to meet you all. Please sit down.

SUPERVISOR. May I stow my relatives in this chair? There's quite a lot of them. (*He puts down his hat, stick and gloves.*)

ISABEL. And to what am I indebted for the pleasure of receiving your family on this occasion?

SUPERVISOR. You haven't guessed? (*He bows ceremonially.*) We have come for the purpose of asking your hand in marriage, Mademoiselle.

ISABEL. But, really . . . !

SUPERVISOR. Not a word, if you please. We ask you for your hand, not for your answer. We ask you, by withholding your answer until tomorrow, to give me the happiest day of my life — a day during which I can say to myself that at last I have asked you, and as yet you have not refused. A day in which I am permitted to think that you may be a little touched, perhaps, by the thought that there is someone, however unworthy, who lives only for you. Someone, incidentally, called Robert — my father (*He takes up the hat.*) will have told you my name by now. Someone who is brave, honest, conscientious, reliable — and even modest. For my grandfather (*He takes up the cane.*) can hardly be expected to spare you even the least of my virtues. Someone who — come, Uncle Albert — (*He takes his gloves.*) has the honor to wish you good day, Mademoiselle. Until tomorrow.

ISABEL. No, no. Don't go. Only — you come at such a moment!

SUPERVISOR. I chose the moment deliberately. It is his moment. And therefore the logical time for me to offer you another road to the other world.

ISABEL. What road is that? Are there more than one?

SUPERVISOR. There is a road which leads slowly, easily, but very surely, to death.

ISABEL. What road?

SUPERVISOR. Life.

2. What is Isabel's physical reaction? What is her tone of voice?

ISABEL. Life with you?[2]

SUPERVISOR. That's not the important thing. I, as an individual, don't count for much in this affair. What I offer you is not so much life with me, as life with a government employee. I offer you a career which ends quite pleasantly in the other world. I suppose I go with it. But perhaps you don't understand me?

ISABEL. I think perhaps I do.

SUPERVISOR. In the civil service, we move from post to post, from year to year, with the smoothness of time. We are borne as on a gentle stream from increment to increment, from youth to age, from age to death, without break and without transition.

ISABEL. It doesn't sound so terribly exciting.

SUPERVISOR. It is immensely exciting. It is all sheer poetry.

ISABEL. Really? I wish you'd explain that to me. You find it all sheer poetry in the Bureau of Weights and Measures?

SUPERVISOR. Say, I am checking the volume of the barrels in a distillery. So many liters, so many liters, so many liters. The moment I am bored—I transform these liters into gallons, and in a twinkling, I am in America. On the way home, I have ten kilometers to travel. If I put it into versts, I am in Russia; in

3. How might the supervisor dramatize his explanation? Which words in his speech would be emphasized?

parasangs, in Persia; in fathoms, I am under the sea.[3]

ISABEL. Oh.

SUPERVISOR. I check a load of grain in hins—the owner becomes an ancient Hebrew; in talents—a Roman; in drachmae—a Greek. I take a height in cubits—I am with Cleopatra; in ells, with Alfred the Great.

ISABEL. You *are* a poet, aren't you?[4]

4. How might Isabel's growing interest be shown during the supervisor's speech?

SUPERVISOR. The poetry of a life like mine is surpassed only by its continual surprises . . . !

ISABEL. Its surprises? Do you have surprises in the Weights and Measures? I should like to understand that. Because, frankly, surprises are what I love best of all in life.

SUPERVISOR. We have the most delightful, the most

exquisite surprises. You know, of course, Miss Isabel, that in my bureau we have to change posts every three years. . . .

ISABEL. It seems rather long to be in one place.

SUPERVISOR. But at the very beginning of each assignment, we are given the names of the two towns from which our next assignment will be drawn.

ISABEL. So you always know where you are going next?

SUPERVISOR. That's just it. I know and I don't know. I know that it will be either Nice or Tours. But I won't know which until the very week I leave. Can you possibly appreciate the delicious torment of this continual uncertainty?

ISABEL. So that every day of the three years you have spent with us, your thoughts have been vibrating between Nice . . .

SUPERVISOR. The beach, the casino, the boardwalk, the sea . . .

ISABEL. And Tours?

SUPERVISOR. The castles, the churches, the plain and the river. Now do you see what life can be? Tell me frankly—between the riddle of life with me, and the riddle of death—with him—which seems the more interesting?

ISABEL. I didn't know about this. It sounds marvelous. So that when you are in Nice . . .

SUPERVISOR. Or will it be Tours . . . ?

ISABEL. You will have three whole years in which to wonder about the next possibility?

SUPERVISOR. Chartres and Grenoble.

ISABEL. The valley and the mountain . . .

SUPERVISOR. And so by a series of pendulum swings involving every earthly possibility—we come at last to . . .[5]

ISABEL. Paris.

SUPERVISOR. Yes.

ISABEL. What a beautiful cruise your life must be! One can see its wake in your eyes!

SUPERVISOR. People talk of sailors' eyes. It's because when they pay their taxes, they never look into the eyes of the collector. It's because when they pass the

5. What gestures and movements would be appropriate to each character during the supervisor's descriptions of his possibilities? How would the characters be positioned in relation to each other?

customs, they never look at the eyes of the official. It's because in a courtroom, it never occurs to a litigant to take the judge's head in his hands, and turn it gently to the light and gaze into his pupils. In the eyes of a government official, believe me, they would see the reflection of an ocean no sailor ever saw. It is the ocean of life, Miss Isabel.

ISABEL. It's true. It's strange. I see it now in yours. It is blue.

SUPERVISOR. And do you like it, Miss Isabel?

ISABEL. I think—I like it very much.

SUPERVISOR. Ah! In that case . . . (*He goes to the door with a decisive air.*).

ISABEL. What are you doing?[6]

SUPERVISOR. Bolting the doors. Locking the windows. (*He goes to the fireplace.*) Shutting the damper. So. The room is now sealed off from the universe. I serve formal notice upon all intruders to keep out. Sit down, Miss Isabel. We have only to wait quietly a few minutes, and we shall be safe.

ISABEL. Oh, but . . .

SUPERVISOR. But be careful, Miss Isabel. No regrets. No reservations. In all likelihood, he is listening. The slightest word may be construed as an invitation.

ISABEL. My poor ghost! (*The bolted door flies open. The* **GHOST** *appears. He is paler and more transparent than before, and rather more appealing.*)[7]

GHOST. I may come in?

SUPERVISOR. You may not come in. The door is locked and bolted.

GHOST. I have the key to the enigma, Isabel! I can tell you everything, Isabel. Isabel—ask this man to leave us.[8]

SUPERVISOR. I regret. That is out of the question.

GHOST. I am speaking to Isabel.

SUPERVISOR. You will notice that Isabel is not speaking to you.

GHOST. Do you fancy that you are protecting her? (*The* **SUPERVISOR** *bows.*) From what?

SUPERVISOR. I don't know. Therefore I must be doubly careful.

6. How would Isabel react to the supervisor's sudden action?

7. Entrances should be timed carefully. What about the ghost might make him appealing?

8. What movements will convince the audience that the ghost is not a solid person? In the following speeches, determine which character is the focus of interest at specific moments. At what points

GHOST. Don't be afraid. I am **not** in the least dangerous.

SUPERVISOR. Perhaps not. But what you represent is dangerous.

GHOST. You mean—Death?

SUPERVISOR. It's your word.

GHOST. You think you can save her from that?

SUPERVISOR. I am quite sure.

GHOST. And suppose I am not alone? Suppose that Death is here with me? Suppose that Isabel sees something that you do not see?

SUPERVISOR. A girl sees all sorts of things that her husband doesn't see. It makes no difference—so long as he's there.

GHOST. Oh. So you are married, Isabel?

SUPERVISOR. Not yet.

GHOST. You are engaged?

SUPERVISOR. The word is a little strong. I have asked Isabel to be my wife and she has not refused. I don't know exactly what you call this relationship. . . .

GHOST. I call it vague.

SUPERVISOR. Then obviously I cannot leave her with you for a moment.

GHOST. And suppose *I* leave, and come back when you're gone?

SUPERVISOR. You won't. You haven't the stamina. You haven't the time. The fact is, you, too, seem a little vague, my friend—you are fading. You grow more transparent by the moment. I don't think that in coming back like this, you are making use of any new-found power. I think you have merely some little residue of human energy—and by the looks of you, it will hardly last you an hour. I warn you, unless you go pretty soon, you are likely to suffer the ultimate indignity of disintegrating before her very eyes. If I were you, I'd make a good exit while I still had the wherewithal.[9]

GHOST. Isabel . . .

SUPERVISOR. If you can pass only through closed doors, I'll be glad to close this one for you.

GHOST. Isabel . . .

might the focus be changed so the scene will not be static?

9. What might Isabel be doing while the supervisor and the ghost speak? What are her reactions to the statements of each? How does she reveal her feelings?

10. How might the
characters be
grouped to show
Isabel's dilemma
pictorially?

ISABEL. Dear Supervisor . . . Tomorrow I will listen to you, I promise. But let me have this moment—this last little moment—with him.

SUPERVISOR. If I should desert you in the face of my enemy, tomorrow you would despise me.

ISABEL. But he has come to give me the answer to the riddle that has troubled me all my life![10]

SUPERVISOR. I'm not in favor of the answers to riddles. A riddle is amusing only while it is a riddle. An answered riddle has no dignity whatever—it becomes an absurdity. What riddle?

ISABEL. The riddle of death.

SUPERVISOR. The death of a star, of an ideal, of a flower?

ISABEL. The death of a man.

SUPERVISOR. That's not even a riddle. Do these trifles interest you? Everyone in the Weights and Measures knows the answer to that. Death is the next step after the pension—it's perpetual retirement without pay. And even if that were a riddle—which it isn't—what makes you think the dead would know the answer? If the dead know any more about death than the living know about life, I congratulate them on their insight. And that's all I have to say.

ISABEL. Well, if you won't go, let him speak in your presence. Perhaps he will?

GHOST. He will not.

ISABEL. You could stop your ears a moment.

SUPERVISOR. I'm sorry, but that is just what I can't do. I am provided with eyelids. But not with ear-lids.

GHOST. Such is the lump of concrete out of which destiny is forced to make spirits!

SUPERVISOR. Don't worry about me, my friend. If there's one thing I'm sure of, it's that when my turn comes I will make a perfectly adequate spirit.

GHOST. Oh, you think so?

SUPERVISOR. When I come to my final assignment, my colleagues will know that I was always dependable as a man and that I can be relied upon as a ghost. They will know that I lived my life fully to the extent of my capacity—that I never flagged in my duty to those I served nor in my devotion to those I loved. They will know that in the years I spent in Isabel's town, I never let a day pass without assuring myself that Isabel was well and happy. They may remember the hour I spent one night scratching out with my penknife the word that someone had painted on her door, the morning when I replaced the broken milk bottles on her doorstep, the afternoon when I saved her mail from being soaked by the rain. They will realize that in my modest way, I did my best always to soften the blows that fortune aimed at her.[11]

ISABEL. Dear Robert . . . !

GHOST. I beg pardon?

ISABEL. Nothing.

GHOST. Why do you say, "Dear Robert"?

ISABEL. Because . . . Why? Do you mind my saying it?

GHOST. Not at all. I thank you for saying it. It shows me where I stand with relation to dear Robert. Thanks very much. You have saved me from committing a great folly, the greatest possible folly. I was about to betray an inviolable secret for the sake of a girl. Luckily she betrayed me first.

ISABEL. But how have I betrayed you?

GHOST. And that's how it always is and how it always will be. And there you have the whole story of young girls.

SUPERVISOR. Now what is he talking about?

GHOST. I am speaking of young girls. Sitting in the park, staring at the passer-by without looking at him; lounging with their bicycles at a railroad crossing, in order to welcome the traveler with a gesture of parting; seated at their windows with a book in the lamplight, a pool of radiance between shadow and shadow; like flowers in summer; in winter, like thoughts of flowers, they dispose themselves so gracefully in the world of men that we are convinced we see in them not the childhood of humanity, but its supreme expression. Between the world of a young girl and the world of the spirit, the wall seems no more than a gossamer; one would say that at any moment, through the soul of a girl, the infinite could flow into

11. The supervisor must dramatize the action he visualizes. Which verbs receive emphasis?

12. To whom would the ghost say this? How would the ghost physically show what he visualizes? What are the supervisor's reactions as the ghost speaks?

the finite and possess it utterly. But all at once . . .[12]

SUPERVISOR. Now, please . . . !

GHOST. The man appears. They watch him intently. He has found some tricks with which to enhance his worth in their eyes. He stands on his hind legs in order to shed the rain better and to hang medals on his chest. He swells his biceps. They quail before him with hypocritical admiration, trembling with such fear as not even a tiger inspires, not realizing that of all the carnivorous animals, this biped alone has ineffective teeth. And as they gaze at him, the windows of the soul, through which once they saw the myriad colors of the outer world, cloud over, grow opaque, and in that moment, the story is over.

SUPERVISOR. And life begins . . .

GHOST. Yes. The pleasure of the bed begins. And the pleasure of the table. And the habit of pleasure. And the pleasure of jealousy — and the pleasure of cruelty.

SUPERVISOR. It's a lie. Don't listen to him, Isabel.

GHOST. And the pleasure of suffering. And last of all, the pleasure of indifference. So, little by little the pearl loses its luster and long before it dies, it is dead.

ISABEL. Oh, Ghost — Ghost . . . ! If this is what life is, save me from it!

GHOST. No, Isabel. Your Supervisor is right. You belong not to us, but to him. You are as false and as shallow as the others. What you really love is not the truth, but the pleasure of vibrating endlessly between two falsehoods, between Nice and Tours. Well, you are welcome to your little game. It is not through you that the riddle will be solved and the miracle accomplished.[13]

13. Between what views of life is Isabel torn? How would her actions reveal her torment?

ISABEL. Oh please — tell me.

GHOST. I will tell you nothing. I will tell you not even the name of the little flower which carpets the fields of death, whose petals I shall bring one day to someone more fortunate than you. Take her in your arms now, Supervisor. Spring that wolf-trap of yours about her — and may she never again escape while she lives!

ISABEL. Oh, please—please! (*She runs into the arms of the* **GHOST**, *who kisses her tenderly, then pushes her away.*)

GHOST. Farewell, Isabel. (*He goes.* **ISABEL** *stands still a moment, then she falls. The* **SUPERVISOR** *runs to her.*)

SUPERVISOR. Doctor! Doctor! Help! Quickly!

from
THE HEIRESS
ACT 1, SCENE 3
Ruth and Augustus Goetz

I t is the 1850's. The action takes place in the richly tasteful front parlor of Dr. Sloper's house on Washington Square in New York City.

Catherine Sloper, a rather plain looking woman in her late twenties, senses that her widowed father despises her because she lacks her mother's vivacity and charm. Lonely and unloved, she allows herself to be swept up in the attentions of a suave fortune hunter, Morris Graves. Dr. Sloper, learning that Catherine wants to marry Morris, is determined to thwart her plans.

In the following scene Dr. Sloper has refused to give Catherine's hand in marriage to Morris. The Doctor and Morris argue. Catherine appears and is pulled into the conflict.

> **MORRIS** (*pleading now*). Doctor, don't you care to gratify your daughter? Do you enjoy the idea of making her miserable?
>
> **DR. SLOPER.** I'm resigned to her thinking me a tyrant for a few months.
>
> **MORRIS** (*rising*). For a few months!
>
> **DR. SLOPER.** For a lifetime, then. She may as well be

miserable that way, as with you.[1]

MORRIS. Ah, you are not polite, sir!

DR. SLOPER. You push me to it, you argue too much.

MORRIS (*comes closer to* **DR. SLOPER**, *who is now near window wall*). Dr. Sloper, I have fallen in love with your daughter. I am not the kind of man you would choose for her . . . and for good reasons . . . I have committed every folly, every indiscretion a young man can find to commit . . . I have squandered an inheritance . . . I have gambled . . . I have drunk unwisely . . . I admit, I confess all these things . . . [2]

DR. SLOPER. I am acting in the capacity of a judge, Mr. Townsend, not your confessor!

MORRIS. I tell you these things myself, Doctor, because I love Catherine, and because I have a great deal at stake.

DR. SLOPER. Then you have lost it. (*Moves toward archway.*)

MORRIS. No, sir.

DR. SLOPER. Just as surely as if you placed your pittance on the losing number. . . . It is over. You have lost. (*He stands at archway, waits for* **MORRIS** *to leave.*)

MORRIS. Don't be to sure of that, sir. I believe if I say the word she will walk out of this house and follow me.

DR. SLOPER. You are impertinent!

MORRIS (*half in archway*). And may I add, Dr. Sloper, if I did not love your daughter as much as I do, I should not have put up with the indignities you have offered me today.

DR. SLOPER. You have only to leave my house to escape them. Good day, Mr. Townsend.

MORRIS. Good day, sir. (**MORRIS** *has put on his hat, and turns to door. Before he reaches it to open it and leave,* **CATHERINE** *calls from top of stairs.*)

CATHERINE (*unseen*). Wait, Morris, wait! (*She runs downstairs and goes to* **MORRIS**.)[3]

DR. SLOPER. *Catherine!*

CATHERINE. You promised me, Morris, you promised you would be respectful when you saw my father![4]

DR. SLOPER. *Catherine!*

1. Two psychological forces oppose each other in this scene. How would the characters be positioned to emphasize the conflict? At what points would they change positions? Movements must seem natural and spontaneous.

2. What gestures and facial expressions would Morris use?

3. How do Morris and Dr. Sloper react individually to Catherine's voice? To her appearance?

4. What vocal quality, movements, and gestures will emphasize her divided allegiances?

5. There are now three characters on stage. How has Catherine's presence changed the stage picture?

6. What is the tempo of the exchanges between Catherine and her father?

CATHERINE (*taking* MORRIS *by arm and leading him back to drawing-room, enters*). What is the matter, Father?[5]

DR. SLOPER. Catherine, you are without dignity!

CATHERINE. I don't care. Why are you angry? Why are you and Morris quarreling? Tell me, please!

DR. SLOPER. Do you wish to make me happy, Catherine?

CATHERINE. Yes, Father, if I can.[6]

DR. SLOPER. You can if you will. It all depends on your will.

CATHERINE (*slowly*). Is it . . . is it to give him up?

DR. SLOPER. Yes, it is to give him up.

CATHERINE. What has he done? What did Mrs. Montgomery tell you?

DR. SLOPER. Nothing I did not know before.

MORRIS (*puzzled, he comes forward*). Mrs. Montgomery . . . ? My sister?

DR. SLOPER. Yes.

MORRIS. What did she say? Have you spoken with her?

DR. SLOPER. She paid me a visit this morning . . . on my invitation.

CATHERINE. You see how painful this is for me, Father; surely you will want me to know your reasons?

DR. SLOPER. He is a selfish idler.

MORRIS. My sister never told you that.

DR. SLOPER. She did not deny it.

CATHERINE. But, Father, I know he loves me.

DR. SLOPER. I know he does not!

CATHERINE. In God's name, Father, tell me what makes you so sure!

DR. SLOPER (*a pause*). My poor child, I can't tell you that —you must simply take my word for it.

CATHERINE. Father, I can't! I can't! I love him! (*Despairing.*) I have promised to marry him, to stay by him, no matter what comes.

DR. SLOPER. So he forearmed himself by getting a promise like that, did he? (*To* MORRIS.) You are beneath contempt!

CATHERINE (*stolidly*). Don't abuse him, Father! (*After a pause.*) I think we shall marry quite soon. (*Stands next to* MORRIS.)

DR. SLOPER (*turns away—starts for his study*). Then it is

no further concern of mine.

CATHERINE. I'm sorry.

MORRIS. Doctor Sloper! (**DR. SLOPER** *stops and turns to him.*) Doctor Sloper, as much as I love Catherine, we cannot marry without your approval. It would bring unhappiness to all of us.

DR. SLOPER. Do you mean that, sir?

MORRIS. Yes.

DR. SLOPER. Then will you put if off, Mr. Townsend?

MORRIS. Put it off?

DR. SLOPER. Yes, for six months. I would like Catherine to go to Europe with me.

CATHERINE. *Europe?*

DR. SLOPER. I would like you very much to go, Catherine.

CATHERINE. Why, Father?

MORRIS. Your father thinks you will forget me, Catherine.

CATHERINE. I don't want to go!

DR. SLOPER. Are you afraid, Catherine? Are you afraid of a six months' separation?

CATHERINE. I shall still love him when I come back.

DR. SLOPER. You are romantic, my dear, and very inexperienced.

CATHERINE. Yes, I am.

DR. SLOPER. And at the moment you are exalted with the feeling of undying devotion to a lover. You are very sure of your love . . . But, Catherine, do you dare test him?

CATHERINE. You underestimate him.

DR. SLOPER. I don't think so. (*Then looks squarely at* **MORRIS.**)

MORRIS (*after pause, goes to* **CATHERINE** *and takes her hand*). Catherine, go to Europe. (*Now he looks squarely at* **DR. SLOPER.**) Go to Europe with your father.[7]

7. How might Morris's voice change when he turns to look at Dr. Sloper?

from
ANTIGONE
Jean Anouilh
(translated by Lewis Galantiere)

This is a modern version of the classical Greek tragedy by Sophocles. The time is the present, with the action taking place in front of King Creon's palace.

Polyneices has been killed while leading an insurrection against King Creon. According to moral law Polyneices should have been buried. To humiliate the traitor's memory, however, Creon prohibited burial. Antigone, Polyneice's sister, ignoring the king's prohibition, has secretly buried her brother's body. She is aware that she must ultimately forfeit her life for her action.

In this scene Antigone meets her fiancé, Haemon, who does not yet know of her crime. Only Antigone knows that they are meeting for the last time.

1. Would Antigone's manner be gay or solemn? Why does she move away from Haemon?

2. Antigone's sister.

ANTIGONE. Haemon, Haemon! Forgive me for quarreling with you last night. (*She crosses quickly to Left of* **HAEMON.**)[1] Forgive me for everything. It was all my fault. (**HAEMON** *moves a few steps toward her. They embrace.*) Oh, I beg you to forgive me.

HAEMON. You know that I've forgiven you. You had hardly slammed the door; your perfume still hung in the room, when I had already forgiven you. (*He holds her in his arms and smiles at her.*) You stole that perfume. From whom?

ANTIGONE. Ismene.[2]

HAEMON. And the rouge, and the face powder, and the dress?

ANTIGONE. Ismene.

HAEMON. And in whose honor did you get yourself up so glamorously?

ANTIGONE. I'll tell you. (*She draws him closer.*) Oh, what a fool I was! To waste a whole evening! A whole, beautiful evening!

HAEMON. We'll have other evenings, my sweet.

ANTIGONE. Perhaps we won't.[3]

HAEMON. And other quarrels, too. A happy love is full of quarrels.

ANTIGONE. A happy love, yes. Haemon, listen to me.

HAEMON. Yes?

ANTIGONE. And don't laugh at me this morning. Be serious.

HAEMON. I am serious.

ANTIGONE. And hold me tight. *Tighter* than you have ever held me. I want all your strength to flow into me. (*They embrace closer. His cheek against her upstage cheek.*)

HAEMON. *There!* With all my strength. (*A pause.*)

ANTIGONE (*breathless*). That's good. (*They stand for a moment, silent and motionless.*) Haemon! I wanted to tell you. You know—The little boy we were going to have when we were married?

HAEMON. Yes?[4]

ANTIGONE. I'd have protected him against everything in the world.

HAEMON. Yes, dear sweet.

ANTIGONE. Oh, you don't know how I should have held him in my arms and given him my strength. He wouldn't have been afraid of anything, Haemon. His mother wouldn't have been very imposing: her hair wouldn't have been very well brushed; but she would have been strong where he was concerned, so much stronger than any other mother in the world. You believe that, don't you, Haemon?[5]

HAEMON. Yes, my dearest.

ANTIGONE. And you believe me when I say that *you* would have had a real wife?

HAEMON (*draws her into his arms*). I *have* a real wife.

ANTIGONE (*pressing against him and crying out*). Haemon, you loved me! You *did* love me that night. You're sure of it![6]

HAEMON. What night, my sweet?

ANTIGONE. And you are sure that that night, at the dance, when you came to the corner where I was

3. What transition in thought occurs here?

4. Does Haemon suspect anything yet? How should his tone reveal his feelings?

5. Which words should be emphasized to reveal Antigone's tension?

6. What emotions cause this outburst?

sitting, there was no mistake? It was *me* you were looking for? It wasn't another girl? And that not in your secret heart of hearts, have you said to yourself that it was Ismene you ought to have asked to marry you?[7]

7. Why does Antigone ask these questions?

HAEMON (*reproachfully*). Antigone, you are idiotic. (*He kisses her.*)

ANTIGONE. Oh, you do love me, don't you? You love me as a woman—as a woman wants to be loved, don't you? Your arms around me aren't lying, are they? Your hands, so warm against my back—they aren't lies? This warmth; this strength that flows through me as I stand so close to you. They aren't lies, are they?

HAEMON. Antigone, my darling—I love you. (*He kisses her again.*)

ANTIGONE (*turns her head partly away from him*). I'm sallow—and I'm not pretty. Ismene is pink and golden. She's like a fruit.

HAEMON. Antigone—!

ANTIGONE. Oh, forgive me, I am ashamed of myself. But this morning, this special morning, I must know. Tell me the truth! I beg you to tell me the truth! When you think of me, when it strikes you suddenly that I am going to belong to you—(*She looks at him.*)[8] do you get the sense that—that a great *empty* space— is being hollowed out inside you; and that there is something inside you that is just—dying?

8. What is the nature of her look?

HAEMON. Yes, I do. (*A pause as they face against one another.*)[9]

ANTIGONE. That's the way I feel. (*She clings to him for a moment.*) There! And now I have two things more to tell you. And when I have told them to you, you must go away instantly, without asking any questions. However strange they may seem to you. However much they may hurt you. Swear that you will! (*A pause, as* **HAEMON** *kisses her hand.*)

9. A transition begins here. How will it affect Antigone's tone of voice and physical manner?

HAEMON (*beginning to be troubled*).[10] What are these things that you are going to tell me?

10. How does Haemon show this?

ANTIGONE. Swear, first, that you will go away without a single word. Without so much as looking at me. (*She looks at him, wretchedness in her face.*) You hear me,

Haemon. Swear, please. It's the last *mad* wish that you will ever have to grant me. (*A pause.*)[11]

HAEMON. I swear it.

ANTIGONE. Thank you. Well, here it is. First, about last night, when I went to your house. You asked me a moment ago *why* I wore Ismene's dress and rouge. I did it because I was stupid. I wasn't sure that you loved me—as a woman; and I did it because I wanted you to want me.[12]

HAEMON. Was *that* the reason?[13] Oh, my poor—

ANTIGONE (*places her hand on his face*). No! Wait! That was the reason. And you laughed at me, and we quarreled. And I flung out of the house. The reason I went to your house last night was that I wanted you to take me. I wanted to be your wife—before.

HAEMON (*questioningly*). Antigone—?

ANTIGONE (*shuts him off; places both hands on his face*). Haemon! You swore you wouldn't ask a single question. You swore it, Haemon. As a matter of fact, I'll tell you why. I wanted to be your wife last night because I love you that way very—very strongly. And also—because— Oh, my beloved— (*She removes her hands from his face.*) I'm going to cause you such a lot of pain. I wanted it also because (*She draws a step away from him.*)[14] I shall never—never be able to marry you, never!

HAEMON (*moves a step toward her*). Antigone—!

ANTIGONE (*she moves a few steps away from him*). Haemon! You took a solemn oath! You swore! Leave me now! Tomorrow the whole thing will be clear to you. Even before tomorrow: this afternoon. (*He makes a slight gesture toward her.*) If you *please*, Haemon, go now. It's the only thing left that you can do for me if you still love me.[15] (*A pause as* **HAEMON** *stares at her. Then he turns and goes out through the arch Right.*

ANTIGONE *stands motionless. In a strange, gentle voice, as of calm after the storm, she speaks:*) Well, it's over for Haemon, Antigone.

11. What might be happening during the pause?

12. What should be revealed about Antigone's character at this point?

13. How does he show his relief?

14. Why does Antigone move away?

15. What are their physical positions? Their facial expressions?

from
ANTIGONE
Jean Anouilh
(translated by Lewis Galantiere)

The play is a modern version of the classical Greek tragedy. This scene is set in King Creon's headquarters. There is a table. (See page 112 for further background.)

Antigone's brother, Polyneices, was killed while leading a rebellion against King Creon. Contradicting the religious laws of burial, Creon forbade interment of the body, hoping thereby to humiliate Polyneices' memory and discourage further rebellions. However, defying the king's prohibition, Antigone has buried the body of her brother. Creon is Antigone's uncle. Though he is a ruthless practical administrator, the king has offered to spare Antigone's life and kill the guards who arrested her if she will promise to be silent about the incident and obey his laws in the future.

In the action previous to the following excerpt, Antigone has challenged Creon's cold, logical authority. Frustrated by her willful idealism, Creon has momentarily lost his cool sobriety. He has twisted Antigone's arm behind her back. As this scene opens, Antigone is on her knees.

ANTIGONE (*moans*). Oh!—
CREON. I should have done this from the beginning. I
  was a fool to waste words. (*He looks at her.*) I may be
  your uncle; but we are not a particularly affectionate
  family. Are we, eh? (*Through his teeth as he twists.*) *Are
  we?* (CREON *twists her left arm so forcibly that* ANTIGONE,
  *wincing with pain, is propelled round below him to the Left
  side of* CREON. *She stands against back of chair Right of
  the table.*) What fun for you, eh? To be able to laugh
  in the face of a king who has all the power in the
  world; a man who has done his own killing in his
  day; who has killed people just as pitiable as you
  are—and who is still soft enough to go to all this

trouble in order to keep *you* from being killed. (*A moment, then:*)[1]

ANTIGONE. Now you are squeezing my arm too tightly. It doesn't hurt any more. (*A pause.* CREON *stares at her, then drops her arm. He goes below the table to the chair at the Left end of table, takes off his cape and places it on the chair.* ANTIGONE *sits on chair Right of table. She looks off toward the Right.*)

CREON. I shall save you yet. God knows, I have things enough to do today without wasting my time on an insect like you. (*He paces to upstage Center, then turns to her.*) But urgent things can wait. I am not going to let politics be the cause of your death. (*He moves down to upper Right end of table.*) For it is a fact that this *whole* business is nothing but politics: the mournful shade of Polyneices, the decomposing corpse, the sentimental weeping and the hysteria that you mistake for heroism, politics—nothing but politics. (*He sits on upstage Right end of table top.*) Look here. I may be soft, but I'm fastidious. I like things clean, shipshape, well scrubbed. Don't think that I am not just as offended as you are by the thought of that—*meat*—rotting in the sun. (ANTIGONE *rises; stands with her back to him.*) In the evening, when the breeze comes in off the sea, you can smell it in the palace, and it nauseates me. But I refuse even to shut my window. It is vile; and I can tell you what I wouldn't tell anybody else: it's stupid, monstrously stupid. But the people of Thebes have got to have their noses rubbed into it a little longer. My God! If it was up to me, I should have had your brother buried long ago as a mere matter of public hygiene. But if the feather-headed rabble I govern are to understand what's what, that *stench* has got to fill the town for a month![2]

ANTIGONE (*turns partly to him*). You are a *loathsome* man!

CREON. I agree. My trade forces me to be. We could argue whether I ought or ought not to follow my trade; but once I take on the job, I must do it properly.

ANTIGONE (*turns fully to face him*). Why do you do it at all?

1. What happens during the pause? What are the characters' facial expressions?

2. How would Creon's tone vary during this speech? What gestures and movements would he use? What should be revealed about his character? How does Antigone react to his ideas?

CREON. My dear, I woke up one morning and found myself king of Thebes. God knows, there were other things I loved in life more than power.

ANTIGONE. Then you should have said no.³

CREON. Yes— Yes, I could have said no. Only, I felt that it would have been cowardly. I should have been like a workman who turns down a job that has to be done. So I said yes.

ANTIGONE. So much the worse for you, then. I didn't say yes. I can say *no* to anything I think vile, and I don't have to count the cost. But because you said *yes* to your lust for power, all that you can do, for all of your crown, your trappings, and your guards—all that you can do is to have me killed.⁴

CREON. Listen to me.

ANTIGONE. If I want to. I don't have to listen to you, if I don't want to. There is nothing you can tell me that I don't know. Whereas, there are a thousand things I can tell you that you don't know. You stand there, drinking in my words. Why is it that you don't call your guards? I'll tell you why. You *want* to hear me out to the end and that's why.⁵

CREON. You amuse me.

ANTIGONE. Oh, no, I don't. I frighten you. That is why you talk about saving me. Everything would be so much easier if you had a docile, tongue-tied little Antigone living in the palace. But you are going to *have* to put me to death today, and you know it. And it frightens you.

CREON. Very well. I am afraid, then. Does that satisfy you? I am afraid that if you insist upon it, I shall have to have you killed. And I don't want to.

ANTIGONE. *I* don't have to do things that *I* think are wrong. If it comes to that, you didn't really want to leave my brother's body unburied, did you? Say it! Admit that you didn't.

CREON. I have said it already.

ANTIGONE. But you did it just the same. And now, though you don't want to, you are going to have me killed. And you call that being a king!

CREON (*stands up; spaces out his words*). Yes, I call *that*

3. What should Antigone's vocal quality and rate of speech reveal about her attitude toward Creon?

4. What is Antigone's tone of voice? How would the characters be positioned?

5. What gestures and facial expressions are needed here and in the following exchanges? What key words and phrases should be stressed? At what points would the characters change positions? When does the focus of interest change?

being a king.

ANTIGONE. Poor Creon! *My* nails are broken, *my* fingers are bleeding, *my* arms are covered with the welts left by the paws of your guards—but *I* am a queen![6]

CREON. Then why not have pity on me, and live? (*He gestures toward offstage up Right Center.*) Isn't your brother's corpse, rotting beneath my windows, payment enough for peace and order in Thebes?

ANTIGONE. No. You said *yes*, and made yourself king. *Now* you will never stop paying.

6. What is revealed about the characters in this and the previous line? How would their respective tones and physical manners emphasize their differences?

OF THEE I SING
ACT 1, SCENE 3
George S. Kaufman and Morrie Ryskind

It is fall of a Presidential election year, late in the afternoon. The scene takes place at the headquarters of a national political party in one of the grander Atlantic City Boardwalk hotels. There is a secretary's desk in a corner of the room.

Because of its particularly poor showing in recent elections, a national political party has sought and found an attractive candidate and an appealing platform. The candidate is a clever, impulsive young man, John P. Wintergreen. To publicize its candidate the party sponsors a beauty contest to select a bride for Wintergreen. One of the girls in the contest has been particularly successful in her attempt to gain Wintergreen's attention. In the following scene the girls have just gone out. Wintergreen is left alone with his secretary, Mary, an efficient, modest young woman.

1. In the sort of comedy of which this scene is an example, gestures, movements, and facial expressions can be as important as the lines they accompany. Timing and an appearance of spontaneity are important. Study the lines of this

(WINTERGREEN, *his nervousness mounting, is left alone in the room. But not quite alone, for at her desk in the corner* MARY TURNER *is quietly working.*)

WINTERGREEN (*as he sees her*). Oh! (*Takes a moment.*) Say! (*She turns.*) You haven't got a drink on you, have you?[1]

MARY. Why, no. I'm sorry.

WINTERGREEN. That's all right. Didn't want it anyhow. (*Pacing.*)

MARY. Little bit nervous?

WINTERGREEN (*whirling*). Who? Me? What have I got

to be nervous about?[2]

MARY. That's what I was wondering. Twenty-four of the most beautiful girls in the country—and you get the winner. Lot of men would like to be in your shoes.

WINTERGREEN. Yeah, but it's my bedroom slippers I'm worrying about. . . . Say, you've been watching them—who do you think it's going to be?

MARY. I couldn't say. Likely to be any one of them.

WINTERGREEN. That's what I was afraid of. But which one? What's your guess?

MARY. Well, don't hold me to it, but I shouldn't be surprised if it were Miss Devereaux.

WINTERGREEN. Devereaux! I thought so! That's the one with the Southern exposure?

MARY. That's Miss Devereaux. She's a good-looking girl, don't you think?

WINTERGREEN (*in heavy Southern accent*). Yes, she's a good-looking gal, all right.

MARY (*falling right into line*). Don't you-all like good-looking gals?

WINTERGREEN. Down Carolina way we're all a-crazy about good-looking gals, but we-all don't like 'em talking that-a-way.

MARY. How do you-all like 'em to talk, sure enough?

WINTERGREEN (*abandons the dialect*). Say, that's terrible, isn't it? If she wins would I have to listen to that all the time?

MARY. But she does it charmingly. And she's very beautiful.

WINTERGREEN. Beautiful, yeah—I like a beautiful girl—they're all right, but—(*He stumbles.*) when a fellow gets married he wants a home, a mother for his children.

MARY. You've got children?

WINTERGREEN. No, no, I mean if I was married. You see, when you're married—well, you know.

MARY. Well, I think Miss Devereaux might listen to reason. And she'd make a very beautiful mother for your children.

WINTERGREEN. Will you stop saying beautiful? I don't

scene with reference to the actions which might be appropriate to them at specific points.

2. How would his voice reveal his nervousness?

know anything about these girls, any of them. What kind of wives they'd make—whether they could sew, or make a bed, or cook. They don't look as though they'd ever had a skillet in their hands. Say, what *is* a skillet?[3]

3. How has Wintergreen's manner changed? What has caused the change?

MARY. You wouldn't have to worry about that in the White House. They have plenty of servants there.

WINTERGREEN. The White House—yeah, but some day we'll have to move out of the White House. Then what? The Old Presidents' Home? There'll be no servants there. She'll *have* to cook.

MARY. Then she'll cook. And like it.

WINTERGREEN. But will *I* like it? Why, the average girl today can't cook—she can't even broil an egg.

MARY. Nonsense! Every girl can cook.

WINTERGREEN (*scornfully*). Every girl can cook—can you?

MARY. I certainly can!

WINTERGREEN. Then what are you doing here?

MARY (*right back at him*). I'm holding down a job! And I can cook, and sew, and make lace curtains, and bake the best darned corn muffins you ever ate! And what do you know about that?

WINTERGREEN. Did you say corn muffins?

MARY. Yes, corn muffins!

WINTERGREEN. Corn muffins! You haven't got one on you, have you?

MARY. I haven't far to go. (*Opens a drawer in her desk.*) It's lunch, but you can have it.

WINTERGREEN. Oh, I couldn't do that!

MARY. Please! (*As he reaches.*) The second from the left is a corn muffin. That's an apple.

WINTERGREEN (*taking muffin*). Well! You must let me take you to lunch some day. (*Samples it.*) Why—it melts in the mouth! It's—it's marvelous.

MARY. And I'm the only person in the world who can make them without corn.

WINTERGREEN. What a muffin! Say, I don't even know your name.

MARY. That's right—you don't.

WINTERGREEN. Mine's Wintergreen.

MARY. I know. Mine's Turner.

WINTERGREEN. Just Turner?

MARY. Mary Turner.

WINTERGREEN (*suddenly*). Say, why in God's name didn't you get into this contest?

MARY. One of the three million?

WINTERGREEN. Well, you know what the first prize is?

MARY. Yeah, can you imagine?

WINTERGREEN. And you get your picture in the paper.

MARY. Having tea on the lawn with the Filipino delegation. And you throwing the medicine-ball at the Cabinet.

WINTERGREEN. Oh, do we have to have a Cabinet?

MARY. What would you throw the medicine-ball at? Me?

WINTERGREEN (*suddenly sobered*). Gosh, it'd be fun with you. We could have a grand time.

MARY (*the Southern accent*). Why, Mr. Wintergreen —

WINTERGREEN. No, I mean it! Listen — I've only got a minute — maybe less than that! I love you! I know it's awful sudden, but in a minute it'll be too late! Let's elope — let's get out of here!

MARY. But — but wait a minute! You don't know me!

WINTERGREEN. I know you better than those girls! (*A gesture.*) You can make corn muffins, and — you're darned cute-looking, and — I love you!

MARY. But I don't know you!

WINTERGREEN. What's there to know? I'm young, I'm a swell conversationalist, and I've got a chance to be President! And besides that you love me!

MARY. But it's absurd! Why, you can't —

WINTERGREEN. The hell I can't! (*He seizes her and starts kissing her.*) It's fate, Mary, that's what it is — fate! (*Kisses her again.*) Why, we were meant for each other — you and me![4]

MARY. You and *I!*

WINTERGREEN. All right, you and I!

4. How would the kiss be managed in order not to appear silly?

from
THE MAN WHO CAME TO DINNER
ACT 1, SCENE 2
Moss Hart and George S. Kaufman

Set originally in the 1930's, the scene may be updated. It is an evening in December. The action occurs in the tasteful but modest living room of a house in a small town in Ohio. There is an entrance hall with outer door.

Sheridan Whiteside is an internationally known drama critic. While in the home of the Stanleys, an unsophisticated Midwestern family, Whiteside has broken his leg and is confined in a wheelchair. He is a reluctant but demanding guest. Maggie Cutler has been Whiteside's private secretary for several years. She is in her late twenties and has recently fallen in love with Bert Jefferson, a newspaper reporter in the small town in which Maggie and Whiteside are marooned. When the following scene begins Maggie is returning from an afternoon with Bert. Sherry is her nickname for Whiteside.

1. What business is needed here?

MAGGIE. Good evening, Sherry. Really Sherry, you've got this room looking like an old parrot-cage. . . .[1] Did you nap while I was out? (**WHITESIDE** *merely glowers at her.*) What's the matter, dear? Cat run away with your tongue? (*She is on her knees, gathering up debris.*)

WHITESIDE (*furious*). Don't look up at me with those great cow-eyes, you sex-ridden hag. Where have you been all afternoon? Alley-catting around with Bert Jefferson?[2]

2. How does Whiteside's speaking manner differ from Maggie's?

MAGGIE (*her face aglow*). Sherry—Bert read his play to me this afternoon. It's superb. It isn't just that play written by a newspaperman. It's superb. I want you

to read it *tonight. (She puts it in his lap.)* It just cries
out for Cornell.[3] If you like it, will you send it to her,
Sherry? And will you read it tonight?

WHITESIDE. No, I will not read it tonight or any other
time. And while we're on the subject of Mr. Jefferson,
you might ask him if he wouldn't like to pay your
salary, since he takes up all your time.

MAGGIE. Oh, come now, Sherry. It isn't as bad as that.

WHITESIDE. I have not even been able to reach you,
not knowing what haylofts you frequent.

MAGGIE. Oh, stop behaving like a spoiled child, Sherry.[4]

WHITESIDE. Don't take that patronizing tone with me,
you flea-bitten Cleopatra. I am sick and tired of your
sneaking out like some lovesick high-school girl every
time my back is turned.[5]

MAGGIE. Well, Sherry— *(She pulls together the library
doors and faces* **WHITESIDE***.)* I'm afraid you've hit the
nail on the head. *(With a little flourish, she removes her
hat.)*

WHITESIDE. Stop acting like Zasu Pitts and explain
yourself.[6]

MAGGIE. I'll make it quick, Sherry. I'm in love.

WHITESIDE. Nonsense. This is merely delayed puberty.

MAGGIE. No, Sherry, I'm afraid this is it. You're going
to lose a very excellent secretary.

WHITESIDE. You are out of your mind.

MAGGIE. Yes, I think I am, a little. But I'm a girl who's
waited a long time for this to happen, and now it has.
Mr. Jefferson doesn't know it yet, but I'm going to
try my darnedest to marry him.[7]

WHITESIDE *(as she pauses).* Is that all?

MAGGIE. Yes, except that—well—I suppose this is what
might be called my resignation—as soon as you've
got someone else.

WHITESIDE *(there is a slight pause).* Now listen to me,
Maggie. We have been together for a long time. You
are indispensable to me, but I think I am unselfish
enough not to let that stand in the way where your
happiness is concerned. Because, whether you know
it or not, I have a deep affection for you.[8]

3. Katherine
Cornell was a
famous actress. The
name of an actress
of today may be
substituted.

4. How would the
characters be
positioned in
relation to each
other?

5. How might
Whiteside's
wheelchair be used
to heighten the
humor of the scene?

6. Zasu Pitts was a
movie actress who
fluttered her hands
in a woebegone
manner.

7. What range of
emotions should
Maggie's voice
suggest?

8. How has
Whiteside's manner
changed? What is
his tone of voice?

MAGGIE. I know that, Sherry.

WHITESIDE. That being the case, I will not stand by and allow you to make a fool of yourself.

MAGGIE. I'm not, Sherry.

WHITESIDE. You are, my dear. You are behaving like a Booth Tarkington heroine. It's—it's incredible. I cannot believe that a girl who for the past ten years has had the great of the world served up on a platter before her—I cannot believe that it is anything but a kind of temporary insanity when you are swept off your feet in seven days by a second-rate, small-town newspaperman.

MAGGIE. Sherry, I can't explain what's happened. I can only tell you that it's so. It's hard for me to believe too, Sherry. Here I am, a hard-bitten old cynic, behaving like *True Story Magazine*, and liking it. Discovering the moon, and ice-skating—I keep laughing to myself all the time, but there it is. What can I do about it, Sherry? I'm in love.[9]

WHITESIDE (*with sudden decision*). We're leaving here tomorrow. Hip or no hip, we're leaving here tomorrow. I don't care if I fracture the other one. Get me a train schedule and start packing. *I'*ll pull you out of this, Miss Stardust. *I'*ll get the ants out of those moonlit pants.[10]

MAGGIE. It's no good, Sherry. I'd be back on the next streamlined train.

WHITESIDE. It's completely unbelievable. Can you see yourself, the wife of the editor of the Mesalia *Journal*, having an evening at home for Mr. and Mrs. Stanley, Mr. and Mrs. Poop-Face, and the members of the Book-of-the-Month Club?[11]

MAGGIE. Sherry, I've had ten years of the great figures of our time, and don't think I'm not grateful to you for it. I've loved every minute of it. They've been wonderful years, Sherry. Gay and stimulating—why, I don't think anyone has ever had the fun we've had. But a girl can't laugh all the time, Sherry. There comes a time when she wants—Bert Jefferson. You don't know Bert, Sherry. He's gentle, and he's unassuming, and—well, I love him, that's all.[12]

9. What is the tone of Maggie's voice? What gestures and movements would she use?

10. What action might accelerate the tempo here?

11. Why has Whiteside's tone changed?

12. Maggie recollects, then her mood shifts. What movements and gestures will help show this change? What are her facial expressions?

WHITESIDE. I see. Well, I remain completely unconvinced. You are drugging yourself into this Joan Crawford fantasy, and before you become completely anesthetized I shall do everything in my power to bring you to your senses.

MAGGIE (*wheeling on him*).[13] Now listen to me, Whiteside. I know you. Lay off. I know what a devil you can be. I've seen you do it to other people, but don't you dare to do it to me. Don't drug *yourself* into the idea that all you're thinking of is my happiness. You're thinking of yourself a little bit, too, and all those months of breaking in somebody new. I've seen you in a passion before when your life has been disrupted, and you couldn't dine in Calcutta on July twelfth with Boo-Boo. Well, that's too bad, but there it is. I'm going to marry Bert if he'll have me, and don't you dare try any of your tricks. I'm on to every one of them. So lay off. That's my message to *you*, Big Lord Fauntleroy.[14] (*And she is up the stairs. Left stewing in his own juice,* **MR. WHITESIDE** *is in a perfect fury. He bangs the arm of his chair, then slaps at the manuscript in his lap. As he does so, the dawn of an idea comes into his mind.*)

13. How can the fact that Whiteside is seated and Maggie is standing be used to focus attention on Maggie? When necessary, how might attention be drawn to Whiteside?

14. Maggie has changed moods again. Her speech must build to a high point. Where does the climax occur?

Courtesy of the William-Alan Landes Collection.
Generation (l to r) Walter (Richard Jordan) and Bolton
(Henry Fonda).

from
GENERATION
ACT 1
William Goodhart

It is the present, a late Saturday afternoon. The scene is set in a large, one-room studio loft in New York City. Furniture is sparse and mostly home-made.

Jim Bolton is a successful advertising executive. He has come to New York from Chicago to meet his new son-in-law, Walter Owen, who is a photographer. He finds that Doris, his daughter, is pregnant. As the scene opens, Bolton is looking at a book of Walter's photographs.

BOLTON. You took all these pictures, huh?

WALTER. Uh-huh.

BOLTON. They're surprisingly good. (**DORIS** *looks significantly at* **WALTER.**)[1]

1. What does the stage direction suggest about the positioning of the three characters?

WALTER (*in response to her prodding*). Thank you.

DORIS (*crossing to kitchen, says to her father*). See! I told you! (*During the following, she continues to prepare dinner.*)

BOLTON (*still looking at the book*). Yes, indeed, *very* good. I may not know the name of my own camera, but I know a good photograph when I see it. I've been dealing with them for years. Uh, Walter, I uh, I don't suppose you'd want to go into advertising photography.

WALTER. God, no!

BOLTON (*quickly*). Yeah, well, that's what I figured. You're right of course. The only reason I mentioned it at all is that I do have all these friends who could get you started.

WALTER. Oh yeah, I'm sure you must have lots of contacts.[2]

BOLTON. Well, these are more than contacts, these are friends who owe me favors for one thing or another. I've saved them up and I can only collect them once, but if you were at all interested, I'd be glad to give them all to you as, well, as a kind of dowry or something . . .

DORIS (*melting*). Oh, Daddy . . .

WALTER (*rises*). Well, that's very nice of you, but I have to go my own way.[3]

BOLTON. Of course you do, and I'm sure that one of these days, you'll actually get started. I really didn't expect you to go against your beatnik religion, but I had to make certain because there is so much money involved. I mean, with my help you could gross over a hundred thousand the first year. Not that I think you should compromise your principles just to give Doris and the baby a better life. (*Rises, glass in hand.*)[4]

WALTER (*crosses to the table and picks up his camera*).[5] Yes, well, I'm glad you're not like those guys who try to get other people to sell out so they won't feel so bad about their *own* sellout.

BOLTON. Yes, and I'm glad your attitude is so *refreshingly different* from that stupid beatnik stereotype.

DORIS. Oh, Daddy, Walter saw through that whole beat thing years before we had even *heard* about it.

(**WALTER** *takes* **DORIS**' *picture as she briefly assumes a comic pose, then he turns and aims the camera at* **BOLTON**.)[6]

BOLTON. Yes, but has he seen through himself yet? (*Defiantly holding the glass up to his mouth.*)

WALTER (*lowers the camera*). Do you believe in the Golden Rule?

BOLTON. Uh, yes.

WALTER. Well, I don't want to do ads unto others because I *hate it* when others do ads unto me. (**WALTER** *crosses up to the cabinet and puts the camera away.*)

BOLTON. Very well put, Walter. That's very biblical of you. Uh, do we have time for another glass of wine?

DORIS. Sure, Daddy.

BOLTON (*pouring himself some more wine*). What makes

2. What is the tone of Walter's voice? Would he be sarcastic toward Bolton, whom he has just met?

3. How would Bolton react to Walter's action?

4. Why does Bolton rise at this point?

5. What possibility for humor does this action offer?

6. How would Bolton's reaction to Walter's action differ from Doris's?

you think you can continue indefinitely as a teenage drop out?

WALTER. I'll admit I've taken a long time to find myself. I had to find Doris first. (**DORIS,** *moved by this, crosses to his side.*)

BOLTON. Well, now that you have her — for better or for worse — it's high time you started making it better.

DORIS. I'm not sure I could stand making it *much* better. (**WALTER** *and* **DORIS** *kiss.*)[7]

7. What is Bolton's reaction to the kiss?

BOLTON. Well, I don't blame you for being afraid to try commercial photography. You'd have to compete with some fantastic photographers. They can do this kind of stuff with their feet.

WALTER (*crossing to* **BOLTON,** *he picks up his book*). But do they *do* it? I mean have you personally ever seen any of these guys' pictures like this . . . (*Shows* **BOLTON** *a picture.*)

BOLTON (*glancing at the picture*). When a man is flying all over the place making two or three hundred thousand a year, he doesn't have time to hang around waiting for some neurotic tuba player to throw up.[8]

8. As the confrontation builds, what methods of attack and defense do the opponents use? When is each on the offensive? On the defensive? How does Doris respond to her father and to her husband?

WALTER (*crossing down Right to put book away*). Well, I'm relieved to hear that. I wouldn't want any of those guys moving in on *my* racket.

DORIS. Daddy, do you know anyone who could help Walter get his book published?

BOLTON. No. (*He and* **WALTER** *pace up and down, trying not to fight. Suddenly* **BOLTON** *blurts.*) We ad men are holding this whole economy together! What do you think of that?

WALTER (*mildly*). I think you're probably right.

BOLTON (*angrily*). Don't be patronizing.

WALTER. I didn't say I liked it!

BOLTON. Well, I didn't say I liked it either, did I?!

DORIS (*brightly*). See, I knew you two were in agreement all along.

WALTER. Yeah, except that *he does* it!

BOLTON. No, I don't, I don't do any of that hard sell stuff any more. I've been moving more into the area of public relations. I have mainly institutional accounts. My things are informative, dignified . . .

Here, I'll show you, I have a little pamphlet right here. (*Crosses to coat on chair and gets pamphlet, comes back and shows it to* **WALTER**.) It's for welcoming and orienting new employees. See, history of the company, portraits of the company officials, brief biographies . . . Say, maybe you'd be interested in taking some of these portraits . . . [9]

WALTER (*spotting something in the pamphlet*). Did you write this? This right here?

BOLTON (*looking*). Uh, yes.

WALTER. My God, you're a public relations genius! (*He reads to* **DORIS**.) ". . . so strong was his devotion to the Company that he didn't have a single absence in the thirty-two years from the day of his employment as stock boy to the day of his self-defenestration as president!!" Self-defenestration!

DORIS. What does it mean?

WALTER. It means that after thirty-two years of perfect attendance, he threw himself out the window.

DORIS. Daddy! To dispose of a man's life with a phrase like *that!*

BOLTON. Well, I probably shouldn't have mentioned it at all, but it was in all the papers and, well, what the hell could I do? As a matter of fact, this was considered very clever handling of the problem. All right, so it's fudging a little. These things happen. You have to live with them.

WALTER (*upset, he crosses to down right, throwing the pamphlet on the table as he passes it*). You have to, we don't.

BOLTON (*losing control of himself*). You're not living, that's why! You're afraid to! You're afraid to get out and take your chances with the rest of us, so you hide down here in your rat-infested ivory tower, and take potshots at everybody else! It's easy, it's fun, and it's *very safe!*

DORIS. Daddy! Stop it! What do you want from him?

WALTER (*calmly*). He wants respect.

BOLTON (*this hits him hard. He stares for a moment, then covers angrily*). Respect! *Don't make me laugh!* You can't afford to show *anyone* any respect! (*He turns and walks upstage.*)

9. How is Bolton's transition of thought shown in his voice and physical manner?

DORIS. Please don't be hurt, Daddy.

WALTER. Well, I'll be glad to *show* you respect, but *true* respect is involuntary.

BOLTON (*turning around, a note of appeal in his voice*). But you don't *know* me! I'm a very liberal-minded man! Aren't I, Doris?

DORIS. Sure you are, Daddy, and you're a *nice* man.

BOLTON. And I'm a *nice* man. All right, so I happened to go into advertising. I'd like to have gone back to school after the war under the GI Bill and become a doctor or something, but I had family responsibilities and they came first![10]

WALTER (*deliberately casual*). You considered becoming a doctor?

BOLTON. Yes. A buddy of mine wanted me to go to medical school with him. (*Turns to* DORIS *with a sudden thought.*) Say, he's an obstetrician. Maybe you should call him. Who do you have now?

WALTER (*cutting in quickly*).[11] Yeah, you should have been a doctor. It's practically the same racket you're in now, public relations. They have a wonderful set-up, you know: they've got all these viruses working for them day and night and they keep the supply of doctors down, see, so there are plenty of viruses to go around. Now, they may not know them all by name, but, I mean, who wouldn't have status with a deal like that? They're *it*, man, the supreme authorities from the cradle to the grave. Why, the very instant a child is born today, it falls right into their hands.

DORIS (*warningly*). Walter! (WALTER *catches himself.*)

BOLTON (*to* WALTER). I would *love* to hear you make one positive, constructive statement of any kind . . .

WALTER (*airily*). Oh, I'm very positive, and I foresee a very constructive future when the doctors take over the whole country. I wrote a thing about it: about this Doctor-Dictator who's in this patriotic religious procession making his traditional annual house call, in this papier-mâché horse and buggy, with the fake snow blowing on him, and he's going along, blessing the crowd with LSD 25. Oh, you'd love this Doctor-

10. Does Bolton believe what he is saying? How would his voice reveal his feelings?

11. Why does Walter cut in quickly? What are his manner and tone of voice?

Dictator, he's very positive.[12]

BOLTON (*indignantly*). I happen to be for socialized medicine!

WALTER. Oh, beautiful! Throw out *their* rotten institution and stick in *your* rotten institution—they're all the same crooked bureaucrats hiding behind you public relations guys! Name me one institution that isn't rotten! Go ahead! Name one!

BOLTON (*after a moment of desperately trying to think of one*). Uh—what about the postal service?[13]

WALTER. Ah, you don't give a damn about them! You just like their slogan— (*Places his hand over his heart and recites mockingly.*) "Neither snow, nor rain, nor heat, nor gloom of night stays these couriers from the swift completion of their appointed rounds". . . .

BOLTON (*turns on* **DORIS** *and shouts angrily*). You've married an anarchist, you know that, don't you?!

DORIS (*rushing to serve the dinner, she says distractedly*). I know, Daddy, but can't we have a nice dinner anyway.

BOLTON (*turning back to* **WALTER**). If you don't believe in anything, what's the idea of marrying my daughter and starting a family?!

WALTER (*passionately*). Because that's the only thing I'm sure of! It's obvious we're supposed to pair off like this, a man and a woman, that's the way we're *made!* And that's why I distrust any group bigger than two! We're not made *that* way!

BOLTON. The point is, you two are already three.[14] And—

WALTER (*interrupting angrily*). Ah, you know as well as I do that the whole setup is rotten, you just don't have the guts to admit it!

BOLTON (*furious*). I have a damn sight more guts than you have! I'm in there fighting to improve it!

WALTER. With what? "Self-defenestration?" Actually, that's just what we need, a new national holiday, Self-Defenestration Day! Clean out the System! (*Jumps.*) Ah-h-h-h-h-h!

DORIS (*crossing to table with salad*). Walter, will you toss the salad? Everything else is ready! (**WALTER** *crosses*

12. How would Walter dramatize his idea? How would Doris and Bolton be reacting?

13. How would Bolton's desperate moment of thought be shown?

14. Where is the emphasis in this line?

Courtesy of the William-Alan Landes Collection.
Generation (l to r) Bolton (Henry Fonda), Walter
(Richard Jordan), and Doris (Holly Turner).

to the table and angrily tosses and serves the salad during the following.)

BOLTON. Oh, this town is just full of you smart-alecs tearing things down, throwing everything out, good, bad, what's the difference to you? Daddy will fix it. And we will. I don't care what you say, I know the *real* men are with *me*—building, repairing, trying to make things better!

WALTER. If you were, if you really were, I'd respect you. But you're not. You're a hypocrite!

BOLTON (*livid*). How dare . . .

WALTER (*interrupting*). You claim you're for socialized medicine and stuff like that, and yet you cheat on your income tax which pays for it! You're such a cheat, you can't even come down to see your own daughter without pulling something cute! (*To* **DORIS.**) You know what he wrote down in his expense book for the trip down here? *Taxi to Photographers!*[15]

DORIS (*shocked*). Daddy! You didn't!

BOLTON. Oh, for God's sake, everybody does that!

DORIS (*takes the empty salad bowl and puts it on the counter*). Daddy, you take the money for our wedding present and you pay your taxes with it.

WALTER. What wedding present?

(**BOLTON** *paces around above the couch.*)

DORIS. Don't get upset, there won't be any. (**DORIS** *crosses and puts her apron away,* **WALTER** *paces down Left.*)

BOLTON. All right, so I won't deduct it! I'll take my dirty advertising money and give it to the tax collector! *He'll* take it! Will that make you happy?!

DORIS (*crosses to table*). You have to be honest for yourself, Daddy. Being honest for other people doesn't count. All right, everybody sit down! (*She sits up Center,* **WALTER** *paces up and down stage Left as* **BOLTON** *paces stage Right.*)[16]

BOLTON. This is ridiculous! Doris, you can't reject me, your own father, just because I deducted a taxi fare!

DORIS. We're not rejecting you, just your money.

WALTER (*sitting on the left stool*). Ignore us financially.

BOLTON. How can I ignore you financially, you're part

15. How should Walter stress these three words?

16. What is Doris doing while the men pace?

of my family! (*He has a sudden insight.*) You *know* I can't ignore you. You *know* I'll keep after you until I force you into the System! And then you can enjoy being rich without feeling guilty! You married my daughter so you'd be *forced* into the System![17]

WALTER (*passionately*). I will not be forced into the System under any circumstances!

BOLTON. You're in it already! You couldn't *exist* without the System, the Water, the Gas, the Police Department, even the doctors! Your child will fall into their hands like everybody else's!

WALTER (*losing control of himself*). No, it won't! Because I'm delivering it right here *myself!* (*He catches himself.*) Oh dammit, I told him!

DORIS. Oh, don't worry darling, he won't say anything.

BOLTON (*incredulously*). Won't say anything.

DORIS (*rises*). If you do anything to spoil this, Daddy, I'll never speak to you again! *I mean that!*

BOLTON. Do you actually expect me to stand by and let you do an insane thing like that! (WALTER *rises.*)

DORIS (*still trying to keep it light*). No, don't stand by — boil water!

BOLTON. You're kidding me.

DORIS (*dropping all effort at pleasantness, says sternly*). I'm not! Daddy, if you won't help I want you to at least promise me you won't interfere. Promise me or I want you to leave right now!

BOLTON. How can I promise a thing like that!

DORIS (*resolutely*). Get his bag. (WALTER *starts to cross up.*)

BOLTON (*seeing she means it, he capitulates*). All right . . . I promise. (WALTER *comes back.*)

DORIS (*embracing her father*). Oh, I knew you'd come through! (*She sits happily.*) Now, let's all have a nice dinner (BOLTON *sits slowly.*)

17. The tempo builds. What facial expressions would be appropriate during the following exchanges?

from
THE BARRETTS OF WIMPOLE STREET
ACT 1
Rudolf Besier

I t is an evening in the fall of 1845. The action is placed in Elizabeth Barrett's bedroom, which also serves as a sitting room. There are a sofa bed, a fireplace, and a window overlooking the street.

The eldest of eleven children, Elizabeth Barrett is an invalid because of a childhood spine injury. Because of her illness, she has been kept virtually a prisoner in her room by her strong-willed widower father who tyrannically dominates the family.

In this scene the Barrett children have gathered in Elizabeth's room, believing that their father will be away for two weeks on business. They are in an elevated mood, and Henrietta is demostrating a spirited dance. The festivities halt abruptly when Dr. Barrett enters unexpectedly. Appearing later in the scene is Wilson, the Barretts' maid.

> **ELIZABETH.** Papa . . . (*An uneasy silence falls.* **HENRIETTA,** *in the middle of the room, stops dead.* **BARRETT** *stands for a moment just beyond the threshold, looking before him with a perfectly expressionless face.*) Good evening, Papa. . . .
> (*Without replying,* **BARRETT** *crosses the room and takes his stand with his back to the fireplace. A pause. No one moves.*)
> **BARRETT** (*in a cold, measured voice*). I am most displeased. (*A pause.*) It is quite in order that you should visit your sister of an evening and have a few quiet words with her. But I think I have pointed out, not once, but several times, that, in her very precarious

Courtesy of Author's Collection. **The Barretts of Wimpole Street** (l to r) Robert Browning (Brian Aherne) and Elizabeth Barrett (Katherine Cornell).

Courtesy of Author's Collection. **The Barretts of Wimpole Street** (l to r) Anabel (Joyce Carey), Bella (Dorothy Mathews), and Elizabeth (Katherine Cornell).

state of health, it is inadvisable for more than three of you to be in her room at the same time. My wishes in this matter have been disregarded—as usual. (*A pause.*) You all know very well that your sister must avoid any kind of excitement. Absolute quiet is essential, especially before she retires for the night. And yet I find you romping around her like a lot of disorderly children. . . . I am gravely displeased. (**HENRIETTA** *gives a nervous little giggle.*) I am not aware that I have said anything amusing, Henrietta?

HENRIETTA. I—I beg your pardon, Papa.

BARRETT. And may I ask what you were doing as I came into the room?

HENRIETTA. I was showing Ba how to polk.

BARRETT. To . . . polk?

HENRIETTA. How to dance the polka.

BARRETT. I see. (*A pause.*)

OCTAVIUS (*nervously*). Well, B-Ba, I think I'll say g-good-night, and—

BARRETT. I should be grateful if you would kindly allow me to finish speaking.

OCTAVIUS. Sorry, sir. I—I thought you'd d-done.

BARRETT (*with frigid anger*). Are you being insolent, sir?

OCTAVIUS. N-no indeed, sir—I assure you, I—

BARRETT. Very well. Now—

ELIZABETH (*quickly, nervously*). As I am really the cause of your displeasure, Papa, I ought to tell you that I like nothing better than a—a little noise occasionally. (*A slight pause.*) It-it's delightful having all the family here together—and can't possibly do me any harm. . . .

BARRETT. Perhaps you will forgive my saying, Elizabeth, that you are not the best judge of what is good or bad for you. . . . And that brings me to what I came here to speak to you about. Doctor Chambers told me just now that you had persuaded him to allow you to discontinue drinking porter with your meals.[1]

ELIZABETH. It needed very little persuasion, Papa. I said I detested porter, and he agreed at once that I should take milk instead.

BARRETT. I questioned him closely as to the comparative

1. How does Barrett's manner with Elizabeth differ from his manner with the other children?

strength-giving values of porter and milk, and he was forced to admit that porter came decidedly first.

ELIZABETH. That may be, Papa. But when you dislike a thing to loathing, I don't see how it can do you any good.

BARRETT. I said just now that you are not the best judge of what is good or bad for you, my child. May I add that self-discipline is always beneficial, and self-indulgence invariably harmful?[2]

ELIZABETH. If you think my drinking milk shows reckless self-indulgence, Papa, you're quite wrong. I dislike it only less than porter.[3]

BARRETT. Your likes and dislikes are quite beside the point in a case like this.

ELIZABETH. But, Papa—

BARRETT. Believe me, Elizabeth, I have nothing but your welfare at heart when I warn you that if you decide to discontinue drinking porter, you will incur my grave displeasure.

ELIZABETH (*indignantly*). But—but when Doctor Chambers himself—

BARRETT. I have told you what Doctor Chambers said.[4]

ELIZABETH. Yes, but—

BARRETT. Did you drink your porter at dinner?

ELIZABETH. No.

BARRETT. Then I hope you will do so before you go to bed.

ELIZABETH. No, Papa, that's really asking too much! I—I can't drink the horrible stuff in cold blood.[5]

BARRETT. Very well. Of course, I have no means of coercing you. You are no longer a child. But I intend to give your better nature every chance of asserting itself. A tankard of porter will be left at your bedside. And I hope that tomorrow you will be able to tell me that—you have obeyed your Father.

ELIZABETH. I am sorry, Papa—but I sha'n't drink it.

BARRETT (*to* **HENRIETTA**). Go down to the kitchen and fetch a tankard of porter.

HENRIETTA. No.

BARRETT. I beg your pardon?

HENRIETTA (*her voice trembling with anger and agitation*).

---

2. What affect does the presence of the other children have on Barrett's manner with Elizabeth?

3. How does Elizabeth show that she is trying to use rational arguments?

4. What would the other children be doing during the conversation? What effect does the conversation have on each of them? How does each show this?

5. What gestures and/or movements are suggested here?

It's—it's sheer cruelty. You know how Ba hates the stuff. The Doctor has let her off. You're just torturing her because you—you like torturing.

BARRETT. I have told you to fetch a tankard of porter from the kitchen.

HENRIETTA. I won't do it.

BARRETT. Must I ask you a third time? (*Suddenly shouting.*) Obey me this instant!

ELIZABETH (*sharply*). Papa . . . Go and fetch it, Henrietta! Go at once! I can't stand this. . . .

HENRIETTA. No, I—

ELIZABETH. Please—please . . . (*After a moment's indecision,* **HENRIETTA** *turns and goes out.*)[6]

BARRETT (*quietly, after a pause*). You had all better say good night to your sister.

ARABEL (*in a whisper*). Good night, dearest. (*She kisses* **ELIZABETH** *on the cheek.*)

ELIZABETH (*receiving the kiss impassively.*) Good night. (**ARABEL** *leaves the room. Then each of the brothers in turn goes to* **ELIZABETH** *and kisses her cheek.*)[7]

GEORGE. Good night, Ba.

ELIZABETH. Good night. (**GEORGE** *goes out.*)

ALFRED. Good night, Ba.

ELIZABETH. Good night. (**ALFRED** *goes out.*)

HENRY. Good night, Ba.

ELIZABETH. Good night. (**HENRY** *goes out.*)

CHARLES. Good night, Ba.

ELIZABETH. Good night. (**CHARLES** *goes out.*)

SEPTIMUS. Good night, Ba.

ELIZABETH. Good night. (**SEPTIMUS** *goes out.*)

OCTAVIUS. G-good night, Ba.

ELIZABETH. Good night. (**OCTAVIUS** *goes out.* **BARRETT**, *standing before the fireplace, and* **ELIZABETH**, *on her sofa, look before them with expressionless faces. A pause.* **HENRIETTA** *enters with a tankard on a small tray. She stands a little beyond the threshold, glaring at her father and breathing quickly.*)

ELIZABETH. Give it to me, please. (**HENRIETTA** *goes to her.* **ELIZABETH** *takes the tankard and is putting it to her lips, when* **BARRETT** *suddenly, but quietly, intervenes.*)

BARRETT. No. (*Putting* **HENRIETTA** *aside, he takes the*

6. What is Henrietta's facial expression as she considers? As she leaves?

7. How might this business be planned so that each shows distinctive behavior?

tankard from **ELIZABETH.** *To* **HENRIETTA.**) You may go.

HENRIETTA. Good night, Ba darling. (*She moves forward to* **ELIZABETH**, *but* **BARRETT** *waves her back.*)[8]

BARRETT. You may go.

ELIZABETH. Good night. (**HENRIETTA**, *with a defiant look at her father goes out.* **BARRETT** *puts the tankard on the mantelpiece; then goes to the sofa and stands looking down at* **ELIZABETH.** *She stares up at him with wide, fearful eyes.*)

BARRETT (*in a gentle voice*). Elizabeth.

ELIZABETH (*in a whisper*). Yes?

BARRETT (*placing his hand on her head and bending it slightly back*). Why do you look at me like that, child? . . . Are you frightened?

ELIZABETH (*as before*). No.

BARRETT. You're trembling. . . . Why?

ELIZABETH. I—I don't know.

BARRETT. You're not frightened of me? (**ELIZABETH** *is about to speak—he goes on quickly.*) No, no. You mustn't say it. I couldn't bear to think that. (*He seats himself on the side of the sofa and takes her hands.*) You're everything in the world to me—you know that. Without you I should be quite alone—you know that too. And you—if you love me, you can't be afraid of me. For love casts out fear. . . . You love me, my darling? You love your father?[9]

ELIZABETH (*in a whisper*). Yes.

BARRETT (*eagerly*). And you'll prove your love by doing as I wish?

ELIZABETH. I don't understand. I was going to drink—

BARRETT (*quickly*). Yes—out of fear, not love. Listen, dear. I told you just now that if you disobeyed me you would incur my displeasure. I take that back. I shall never, in any way, reproach you. You shall never know by deed or word, or hint, of mine how much you have grieved and wounded your father by refusing to do the little thing he asked. . . .

ELIZABETH. Oh, please, please, don't say any more. It's all so petty and sordid. Please give me the tankard.

BARRETT (*rising*). You are acting of your own free will,

---

8. How would Elizabeth react to this?

9. How does Elizabeth react during Barrett's declarations?

and not—[10]

ELIZABETH. Oh, Papa, let us get this over and forget it! I can't forgive myself for having made the whole house miserable over a tankard of porter. (*He gives her the tankard. She drinks the porter straight off.* **BARRETT** *places the tankard back on the mantelpiece; then returns to the sofa and looks yearningly down at* **ELIZABETH.**)

BARRETT. You're not feeling worse tonight, my darling?

ELIZABETH (*listlessly*). No, Papa.

BARRETT. Just tired?

ELIZABETH. Yes . . . just tired.

BARRETT. I'd better leave you now. . . . Shall I say a little prayer with you before I go?

ELIZABETH. Please, Papa. (**BARRETT** *kneels down beside the sofa, clasps his hands, lifts his face, and shuts his eyes.* **ELIZABETH** *clasps her hands, but keeps her eyes wide open.*)

BARRETT. Almighty and merciful God, hear me, I beseech Thee, and grant my humble prayer. In Thine inscrutable wisdom Thou hast seen good to lay on Thy daughter Elizabeth grievous and heavy afflictions. For years she hath languished in sickness; and for years, unless in Thy mercy Thou take her to Thyself, she may languish on. Give her to realise the blessed word that Thou chastisest those whom Thou lovest. Give her to bear her sufferings in patience. Give her to fix her heart and soul on Thee and on that Heavenly Eternity which may at any moment open out before her. Take her into Thy loving care tonight; purge her mind of all bitter and selfish and unkind thoughts; guard her and comfort her. These things I beseech Thee for the sake of Thy dear Son, Jesus Christ. Amen.[11]

ELIZABETH. Amen.

BARRETT (*rising to his feet, and kissing her forehead*). Good night, my child.—

ELIZABETH (*receiving his kiss impassively*). Good night, Papa. (**BARRETT** *goes out.* **ELIZABETH** *lies motionless, staring before her for a moment or two. A knock at the door.*) Come in. (**WILSON** *enters, carrying* **FLUSH.**)[12]

10. How is this transition shown in the tone of Barrett's voice and his physical manner?

11. What is Elizabeth's attitude toward the prayer? How would it be shown during the prayer?

12. Flush is Elizabeth's dog.

WILSON (*putting* **FLUSH** *in his basket*). Are you ready for your bed now, Miss Ba?

ELIZABETH. Oh, Wilson, I'm so tired—tired—tired of it all.—Will it never end?

WILSON. End, Miss?

ELIZABETH. This long, long, gray death in life.

WILSON. Oh, Miss Ba, you shouldn't say such things!

ELIZABETH. No, I suppose I shouldn't. . . . Did Flush enjoy his run?

WILSON. Oh, yes, Miss. (*A short pause.*)

ELIZABETH. Is it a fine night, Wilson?

WILSON. Yes, Miss, and quite warm, and there's such a lovely moon.

ELIZABETH (*eagerly*). A moon! Oh, do you think I can see it from here?

WILSON. I don't know, I'm sure.

ELIZABETH. Draw back the curtains and raise the blind. (**WILSON** *does so; and moonlight, tempered by the lamplight, streams on* **ELIZABETH'S** *face.*)

WILSON. There you are, Miss! The moon's right above the chimleys. You can see it lovely!

ELIZABETH (*dreamily*). Yes. . . . Yes. . . . Please put out the lamp and leave me for a little. I don't want to go to bed quite yet.

WILSON. Very well, Miss Ba. (**WILSON** *extinguishes the lamp and goes out.* **ELIZABETH** *is bathed in strong moonlight. She stares, for a while, with wide eyes at the moon. Then her quickened breathing becomes audible, and her whole body is shaken with sobs. She turns over on her side and buries her face in her arms. The only sound is her strangled weeping as the scene closes.*)

from
THE BARRETTS OF WIMPOLE STREET
ACT 4
Rudolf Besier

It is winter, 1845, Elizabeth Barrett's bedroom-sitting room. (See page 136 for further background.)

Elizabeth Barrett has fallen in love with Robert Browning, a poet who generates around him a sense of spontaneity and deep, abundant life. Henrietta, Elizabeth's younger sister, has also fallen in love. She meets secretly with Captain Cook when her father, Dr. Barrett, is out of the house. Cook, a friend of her brother, Octavius, is a frank but somewhat rigid and formal officer in the British Army. Neither of the young women feels that she can reveal her romance to their father, a strict and self-righteously moralistic man.

In the scene which follows, Dr. Barrett has come home and found Henrietta buckling Captain Cook's sword. Annoyed, Barrett sends Cook away, refusing to allow Henrietta to see Cook to the door.

BARRETT (*in silence, he crosses to the fireplace and takes up his stand in front of it. When he speaks he looks straight before him*). Your list of gentlemen visitors appears to be lengthening, Elizabeth.

ELIZABETH. This is the first time I have had the pleasure of meeting Captain Cook.

BARRETT. Indeed. But I infer, from what I saw as I came into the room, that Henrietta's acquaintance is of somewhat longer standing? Or am I mistaken?

HENRIETTA. I have known Captain Cook for some time now.

BARRETT. Ah. And since when has it been your custom to buckle on his accoutrements?

HENRIETTA. I have never seen him in uniform before.

BARRETT. And I think it improbable that you will see him in uniform, or in mufti, very frequently in the future.

HENRIETTA (*in a strained voice*). Why?

BARRETT (*ignoring the question*). Again I may be mistaken, but I was under the impression, Elizabeth, that notice should be given me before strangers visited you here.

ELIZABETH. One can hardly describe a friend of George and Occy as a stranger, Papa.

HENRIETTA. Is Captain Cook to be forbidden the house because I helped him on with his sword?

BARRETT (*to* **ELIZABETH,** *ignoring* **HENRIETTA**). You received my letter?

ELIZABETH. Yes, Papa.

BARRETT. What has just happened fully confirms me in the wisdom of my decision. This house is fast becoming a *rendezvous* for half London. I have neither time nor inclination to find out whether all the persons visiting here are desirable acquaintances for my children. Fortunately our new home is so far from town that your London friends are not likely to trouble us—at least, during the winter.[1]

HENRIETTA (*blankly*). Our new home? . . .

BARRETT (*to* **ELIZABETH**). You have not told your sisters?

ELIZABETH. Arabel knows.

HENRIETTA. I don't understand. Are we—are we leaving Wimpole Street?

BARRETT (*without looking at* **HENRIETTA**). I have taken a house at Bookham, in Surrey. And we move in on the twenty-second.

HENRIETTA. Why?

BARRETT. I am not in the habit of accounting for my actions to any one—least of all, to my children.

HENRIETTA. But one thing I have a right to ask you, Papa. If Captain Cook is to be forbidden to visit us, is it because you found him here in Ba's room and saw

1. How do Elizabeth and Henrietta react individually during Barrett's speech?

me fastening on his sword?

BARRETT (*after a slight pause, looking fixedly at her*). I understood you to say that Captain Cook is George's friend and Occy's.

HENRIETTA. Yes . . . and my friend too.

BARRETT. Ah.

HENRIETTA. Yes, and since it was I who suggested his seeing Ba, and I who asked him to show me how to buckle on his sword, it's unjust to penalise him for —

ELIZABETH (*warningly*). Henrietta . . .

BARRETT (*to* **HENRIETTA** *in a sharp low voice*). Come here.

HENRIETTA (*she takes a few steps towards him, and speaks, a little breathlessly*). Yes, Papa . . . ?

BARRETT (*looks at her steadily under lowered brows for a moment, then points to the floor at his feet*). Come here. (*She goes right up to him, breathing quickly and fearfully. He keeps his eyes fixed on her face. Then in a low, ominous voice.*) What is this fellow to you?[2]

HENRIETTA. I — I've told you. . . . He's a friend of ours.

BARRETT. What is he to *you*?

HENRIETTA. A — a friend. . . .

BARRETT. Is that all?

HENRIETTA. Yes.

BARRETT (*suddenly grasping her wrist, his voice like the crack of a whip*). You liar!

ELIZABETH (*sharply*). Papa!

HENRIETTA (*gaspingly*). Let me go!

BARRETT (*tightening his grip*). What's this man to you? Answer me. (*She tries to free herself and cries out.*) Answer me.

HENRIETTA. Oh, Papa . . . please . . .

BARRETT. Answer me.

HENRIETTA. Oh, don't . . . don't . . .

BARRETT. Answer me.

HENRIETTA (*in a strangled voice*). He's — he's — oh, Papa, I love him —

BARRETT. Ah . . . (*between his teeth, seizing her other wrist and forcing her to her knees.*) ah — you — you — you — (*She gives a cry of pain.*)

2. What is Henrietta's facial expression?

ELIZABETH (*seizing* BARRETT'S *arm*). Let her go, Papa! I won't have it! Let her go at once! (BARRETT *flings* HENRIETTA *off. She collapses in a heap on the floor, sobbing, her face buried in her hands.*)

BARRETT (*turning on* ELIZABETH). And you—you knew of this—filthiness?

ELIZABETH. I've known for some time that Henrietta loved Captain Cook, and I've give her all my sympathy.

BARRETT. You dare to tell me—

ELIZABETH. Yes. And I would have given her my help as well, if I had had it to give.

BARRETT. I'll deal with you later. (*To* HENRIETTA.) Get up.

HENRIETTA (*suddenly clasping his knees and speaking in a voice of passionate entreaty*). Oh, Papa, please listen to me—please. I—I'm not a bad girl—I swear to you I'm not. I know I've deceived you—and I'm sorry—I'm sorry. . . . But I couldn't help it. I—I love him—we love each other—and if you'd known you would have turned him from the house. . . . Oh, can't you understand—won't you try to understand? . . . He's poor—we don't expect to be married yet—but he's a good man—and it can't be wrong to love him. Other women love—why must I be forbidden? I want love—I can't live without love. Remember how you loved Mamma and how she loved you—and—and you'll understand and pity me. . . .[3]

BARRETT (*inexorably*). Get up.

HENRIETTA. Have pity on me, Papa. . . .

BARRETT. Get up. (*He forcibly loosens her hold of his knees, and she staggers to her feet.*) Sit there. (*He points to a chair. She drops into it, and sits listlessly with drooped head.*) How long has this been going on? (HENRIETTA *says nothing.*) Do you hear me? How long have you been carrying on with this fellow?

HENRIETTA. I—I've known him a little over a year.

BARRETT. And you've been with him often?

HENRIETTA. Yes.

BARRETT. Alone?

3. Why does Henrietta beg forgiveness after Barret's cruelty?

HENRIETTA. Yes.

BARRETT. Where?

HENRIETTA. We—I—I've met him in the Park, and—and—

BARRETT. And—here?

HENRIETTA. Yes.

BARRETT. Here. And alone? (**HENRIETTA** *is silent.*) Have you met him in this house alone?

HENRIETTA. Yes.

BARRETT. So! Furtive unchastity under my own roof—and abetted by one whom I believed to be wholly chaste and good. . . .[4]

HENRIETTA. No—no—

ELIZABETH (*fiercely*). How dare you, Papa!

BARRETT. Silence! (*To* **HENRIETTA**, *his voice hard and cold as ice.*) Now attend to me. Something like this happened a year or two ago, and I thought I had crushed the devil in you then. I was wrong. It needed sterner measures than I had the courage to use. . . . So now, unless I have your solemn word that you will neither see nor in any way communicate with this man again, you leave my house at once, as you are, with nothing but the clothes you have on. In which case, you will be your own mistress, and can go to perdition any way you please. But of this you may be certain. Once outside my doors you will never again be admitted, on any pretext whatever, so long as I live. I think by this time you have learnt that it's not my habit to make idle threats, and that I never go back on my word. Very well. You have your choice. Take it.

HENRIETTA (*after an agonised mental struggle*). Is it nothing to you that I—that I shall hate you for this to the end of my life?[5]

BARRETT. Less than nothing.

HENRIETTA. But—but I must let Captain Cook know that—

BARRETT. I will deal with Captain Cook.

HENRIETTA (*desperately*). But Papa—

BARRETT. Will you give me your word neither to see

4. Over-acting will make Barrett melodramatic. Care must be taken to handle the characters with honesty. How has Elizabeth been reacting during the exchanges between Henrietta and Barrett?

5. What is the nature of Henrietta's struggle? How would her struggle affect her speech and physical manner?

Courtesy of Author's Collection. **The Barretts of Wimpole Street** (l to r) Edward Moulton-Barrett (Charles Waldron) and Elizabeth (Katherine Cornell).

nor to communicate with this man again?

HENRIETTA (*after a pause, in a dead voice*). I—I have no choice.

BARRETT. Give me your Bible, Elizabeth.

6. What is the tone of this single word?

ELIZABETH. Why?[6]

BARRETT. I am not prepared to accept your sister's bare promise. But I think even she would hesitate to break an oath made with her hand resting on the Word of God. Give me your Bible.

7. How can Elizabeth's emotional state be portrayed vocally?

ELIZABETH. My Bible belonged to Mamma. I can't have it used for such a purpose.[7]

BARRETT. Give me your Bible.

ELIZABETH. No.

8. What is the tone of Barrett's voice?

BARRETT. You refuse?[8]

ELIZABETH. Yes.

9. What is the facial expression of each character as the scene ends? How would they be positioned on the stage?

(**BARRETT** *pulls the bell rope.*)[9]

from

THE BARRETTS OF WIMPOLE STREET

ACT 5, SCENE 1

Rudolf Besier

It is winter, 1845. The action is set in Elizabeth Barrett's bedroom-sitting room. (See pages 136 and 143 for further background.)

Elizabeth Barrett plans to marry secretly the poet Robert Browning and to go to Italy with him. She must marry secretly because she knows that her father, Dr. Barrett, a strict and moralistic man, would surely forbid and prevent the marriage. Elizabeth has long been an invalid due to a childhood spinal injury, but also in great part because of her father's need to dominate her and keep her near him. As her love for Browning has developed, however, her health has improved amazingly. Henrietta, Elizabeth's younger sister whom Dr. Barrett had forced to swear never again to see her own lover, Captain Cook, plans also to break her oath and marry.

Barrett, angered by a sudden defiance in Elizabeth's attitude toward him, has refused to see or speak to Elizabeth for the past ten days. In the present scene, unable to maintain his silence any longer, Barrett appears in Elizabeth's room.

BARRETT. Do you know why I am back so early?

ELIZABETH (*in a whisper*). No, Papa.

BARRETT (*in a low, intense voice*). Because I could bear it no longer. . . . It's ten days since last I saw you. . . .

ELIZABETH. Am I to blame for that, Papa?[1]

BARRETT (*with restrained fury*). You dare to ask me such a question? Weren't you a party in your sister's shameless conduct? Haven't you encouraged her? Haven't you helped her? Haven't you defended her?

1. How do Elizabeth's volume, pitch, rate of speech compare to Barrett's?

And did you expect to go scot-free of my displeasure? (*Stopping himself with a violent gesture.*) I've not come to speak about that—but to put it behind me—to forget it—to forget it. . . . I wonder, my child, have you been half so miserable these last ten days as your father?

ELIZABETH. Miserable, Papa?

BARRETT. Do you suppose I'm happy when I'm bitterly estranged from all I love in the world? Do you know that night after night I had to call up all my will power to hold me from coming here to forgive you?[2]

ELIZABETH. Papa—

BARRETT. All my will power, I tell you—all my sense of duty and right and justice. . . . But today I could bear it no longer. The want of your face and your voice became a torment. I had to come. I am not so strong as they think me. I had to come. And I despise myself for coming—despise myself—hate myself. . . .[3]

ELIZABETH. No—no! (*Suddenly rises and puts her hands on his shoulders.*) Oh, Papa, can't you see, won't you ever see, that strength may be weakness, and your sense of justice and right and duty all mistaken and wrong?

BARRETT (*hoarsely, taking her hands from his shoulders*). Mistaken and wrong? What do you mean? . . . (*Quickly stopping her from speaking.*) No, be silent. Don't answer me. . . . Mistaken and wrong? You don't know what you're saying.

ELIZABETH. If you'll only listen to me, Papa, I—

BARRETT. No.

ELIZABETH. But, Papa—

BARRETT. No. (*He moves to the window and stands there, his face half averted from her. A pause. He turns.*) If there were even a vestige of truth in what you say, my whole life would be a hideous mockery. For always— through all misfortunes and miseries—I've been upheld by knowing, beyond a doubt, what was right, and doing it unflinchingly, however bitter the consequences. . . . And bitter they've been—how bitter, only God knows! It's been my heavy cross that those

2. How would Barrett move?

3. What does this confession reveal about Barrett?

whom I was given to guide and rule have always fought against the right that I knew to be the right — and was in duty bound to impose upon them. . . . Even you. Even your mother.[4]

ELIZABETH (*in a whisper*). My mother?

BARRETT. Yes, your mother. . . . But not at first. . . . You — you, my eldest child, were born of love and only love. . . . But the others — long before they came the rift had begun to open between your mother and me. Not that she ever opposed me — never once. Or put into words what she felt. She was silent and dutiful and obedient. But love died out — and fear took its place — fear. . . .

ELIZABETH (*sharply*). No! No!

BARRETT. And all because I saw the right — and did it.

ELIZABETH (*in a low voice, staring before her*). Oh . . . oh, dear God, what she must have suffered.

BARRETT. She? — She? . . . And what of me? What of me?[5]

ELIZABETH. You? . . . Oh, Papa, then you — you still loved her — after her love for you had died?

BARRETT (*in a muffled voice, looking aside*). Love? . . . What's love? . . . She was my wife. . . . You — you don't understand. . . .[6]

ELIZABETH (*in a horrified whisper*). And all those children . . . born in fear. . . . Oh, it's horrible — it's horrible — it's horrible. . . . (*With a shuddering sob, she covers her face with her hands.*)

BARRETT (*aghast and embarrassed*). Ba, my dear — don't — don't . . . I — I shouldn't have spoken — I shouldn't have told you all that. . . . Forget it, child. . . . (*He goes up to her.*) Take your hands from your face. . . . (*He gently touches her wrists. She starts away from him, looking at him with wide, frightened eyes.*) Don't look at me like that. (*In a low, thick voice, averting his eyes.*) You don't understand. How should you? You know nothing of the brutal tyranny of — passion, and how even the strongest and best are driven by it to hell. Would you have abetted your sister in her —

ELIZABETH (*fiercely*). Henrietta's love — how dare you speak of it in the same breath as —

4. What is Barrett's ne of voice? His physical manner? What gestures and facial expressions would he use?

5. What should this response reveal about Barrett?

6. How does Barrett's vocal quality vary through this passage?

BARRETT (*brutally*). Her *love? You* ignorant little fool! What do *you* know of love? Love! The lust of the eye—the lowest urge of the body—

ELIZABETH (*springing to her feet*). I won't listen to you!

BARRETT (*seizing her wrist and forcing her back to her seat*). You must—you shall! It's time a little reality were brought into your dream of life. Do you suppose I should have guarded my house like a dragon from this so-called love if I hadn't known, from my own life, all it entails of cruelty and loathing and degradation and remorse? . . . (*He pulls himself together.*) With the help of God, and through years of tormenting abstinence, I strangled it in myself. And so long as I have breath in my body, I'll keep it away from those I was given to protect and care for. You understand me?[7]

7. How does Barrett's tone of voice and physical manner change during this speech?

ELIZABETH (*in a low voice, looking him full in the face*). Yes—I understand you . . . I understand you. . .

BARRETT. Very well. (*A pause.* **ELIZABETH** *sits quite still, looking before her. When he speaks again his voice has changed.*) This has been a hateful necessity. I had to speak—plainly—lest your very innocence should smirch the purity I am utterly resolved to maintain in my home. . . . And because I feel that you acted in innocence and ignorance, I—I forgive you freely, my child. . . . We must turn over this ugly page—and forget what was on it. . . . (*He takes her hand.*) You're—cold as ice. . . . Why are you trembling?

ELIZABETH (*drawing her hand from his*). I shall never forget what you have said.[8]

8. How has Elizabeth's attitude toward Barrett changed? How would this be revealed in the tone of her voice and her physical manner?

BARRETT. Never forget—but—And yet, perhaps that's as well. . . . (*With sudden urgency.*) But, for God's sake, my darling, don't let this raise any further barrier between us! I've told you how all these past months I've seemed to feel you slipping little by little away from me. . . . Your love is all I have left to me in the world.

ELIZABETH. You had Mamma's love once. You might have had the love of all your children.

BARRETT. Yes, if I'd played the coward's part, and taken the easier way, and shirked my duty. I'd rather be hated by the whole world than gain love like that.

ELIZABETH (*in a broken voice*). Oh, Papa, you—you don't know how I pity you. . .

BARRETT (*roughly*). Pity? I don't want your pity. . . . But if I should ever lose you or your love— (*He seizes her unwilling hands.*) My darling, next week we shall have left this house, and I hope we shall never return here. I've grown to loathe it. In our new home we shall draw close to each other again. There will be little to distract you in the country—nothing and no one to come between us. (*He draws her stiffening form into his arms.*) My child, my darling, you want me to be happy. The only happiness I shall ever know is all yours to give or take. You must look up to me, and depend on me, and lean on me. You must share your thoughts with me, your hopes, your fears, your prayers. I want all your heart and all your soul. . . . (*He holds her passionately close; she leans away from him, her face drawn with fear and pain.*)[9]

ELIZABETH (*sobbingly*). I can't bear it— I can't bear any more. . . . Let me go. Papa—please let me go. . . . (*He loosens his embrace, and she falls away from him, her arm covering her face. He rises and bends over her.*)

BARRETT. Forgive me, dear. I've said too much. I was carried away. I'll leave you now.

ELIZABETH (*in a whisper*). Please . . .

BARRETT. Shall I see you again tonight?

ELIZABETH (*as before*). Not tonight.

BARRETT. I shall pray for you.

ELIZABETH (*half to herself*). Pray for me? . . . Tonight. . . . (*She turns and looks up at him.*) Yes, pray for me tonight—if you will. . . . (*He kisses her forehead gently, and goes out. She sits for a moment looking before her, and then, with frightened eyes, round the room. She whispers.*) I must go at once—I must go—I must go. . . . (*She gets up quickly, and fetches her cloak and bonnet from the wardrobe.*)

9. Practicing this final situation in pantomime may help actors determine whether their reaction patterns are honest and not contrived. Over-acting can destroy the intensity of this scene.

PERFORMANCE ONE
Monologues for Women

PLAYING THE GAME
New Theatre Games

Fall 1992

SCENES for ACTING AND DIRECTING   vol. 2

SELECTIONS FROM SHAKESPEARE
(Monologues and Scenes)

Fall 1993

SCENES for ACTING AND DIRECTING   vol. 3

Available from book stores or directly from:
PLAYERS PRESS
P.O. Box 1132
Studio City, CA 91614-0132
U.S.A.